# FeltCraft

Also by Petra Berger (with Thomas Berger):

*The Gnome Craft Book*

*Crafts Through the Year*

*The Easter Craft Book*

Petra Berger

# FeltCraft

## Making Dolls, Gifts and Toys

Floris Books

Translated by Polly Lawson
Photographs by Wim Steenkamp and Thomas Berger
Illustrations by Ronald Heuninck

First published in Dutch under the title *Spelen met vilt* by Christofoor Publishers in 1994
First published in English in 1994 by Floris Books
This edition published in 2010 by Floris Books


www.florisbooks.co.uk



British Library CIP Data available
ISBN 978-0-86315-720-2
Printed in Singapore

# Contents

# Introduction

Felt is a splendid material for working with:

- children can work with it easily
- it is strong and firm
- it can be cut out easily into different shapes
- it does not fray

There are different kinds of felt on the market: from synthetic and half-synthetic to pure woollen felt. Generally the synthetic felt is not satisfactory because it is very thin and the threads are too loosely woven, so while it is being sewn it can easily come apart.

Pure woollen felt, available in a variety of colours, is quite expensive. However the items in this book are generally small so you will only need small pieces.

When you are making dolls, choose the colours with care. Try to give each doll its own character by using the right colour and avoid simply standardizing the colour scheme.

When making objects for young children try to make a true image: for example, do not hang elephants or cars on a mobile because they do not belong there, but birds, butterflies and fairies do.

The patterns in this book are all small. It is better not to use pins as this causes the material to rumple and spoils the shape. Sometimes it is better to tack two layers of felt together before cutting them out.

The patterns throughout this book are drawn to full scale. It is best to cut them out generously as they can easily be trimmed.

## Embroidery stitches

Figure 1 shows a number of stitches which can be used with felt. The simple stitches are usually used to sew pieces together.

Tacking-stitch is used frequently for gathering and for embellishing tapestry, as well as for tacking.

In general back-stitch is used to sew two parts together. Sometimes you can use blanket or buttonhole-stitch for this but that causes a little edge to stand up (see the little dog with the finger puppets on page 31). For the scissor case (page 89) this is used for decoration.

Cross-stitch is really a kind of back-stitch. Half cross-stitch is used in this book for sewing balls together (see page 79). Of course cross-stitch is also used a lot for embellishing. The other stitches shown in Figure 1 are used for decoration, for example in the tapestries (pages 69–77).

## Making hair

The simplest hairstyle is made from thinly-teased unspun wool or carded fleece. Drape the wool over the head. On dolls made of wood glue the wool to the head, but on dolls made of soft fabric sew it on.

With three very thin strands of wool you can also make a plait.

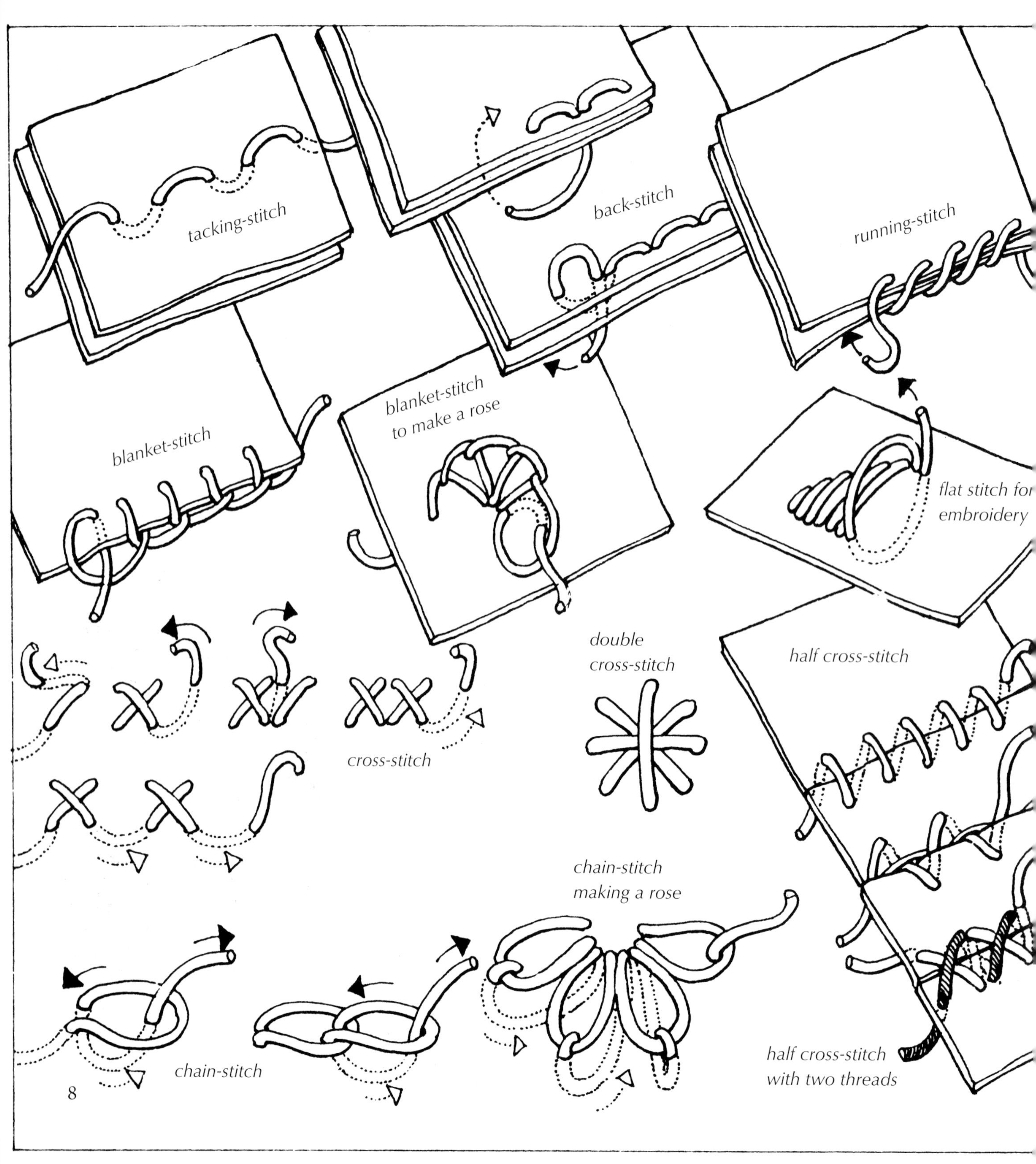

tacking-stitch
back-stitch
running-stitch
blanket-stitch
blanket-stitch
to make a rose
flat stitch for
embroidery
double
cross-stitch
half cross-stitch
cross-stitch
chain-stitch
making a rose
chain-stitch
half cross-stitch
with two threads

With thin knitting wool you can make many more variations. The female doll in Figure 38 has hair with a parting. To achieve this, wind the thin knitting wool twenty or thirty times around two or three of your fingers. Take the wool off your fingers and run a tacking-thread in and out through the strands a few times to bind them together. Glue the hair on to the wooden head and cut through the loops. You will need to sew the hair on to a head made of soft fabric.

For the *mop hairstyle* in Figure 46, first tack the yarns firmly together, but then pull the tacking threads hard together so that from one point the hair stands up in all directions.

For curly hair make wool into separate loops, sew each loop on with a little stitch, and then make the next loop.

For embroidered hair, start at the crown and stitch downwards.

1 *Embroidery stitches (left)*

2 *Making hair*

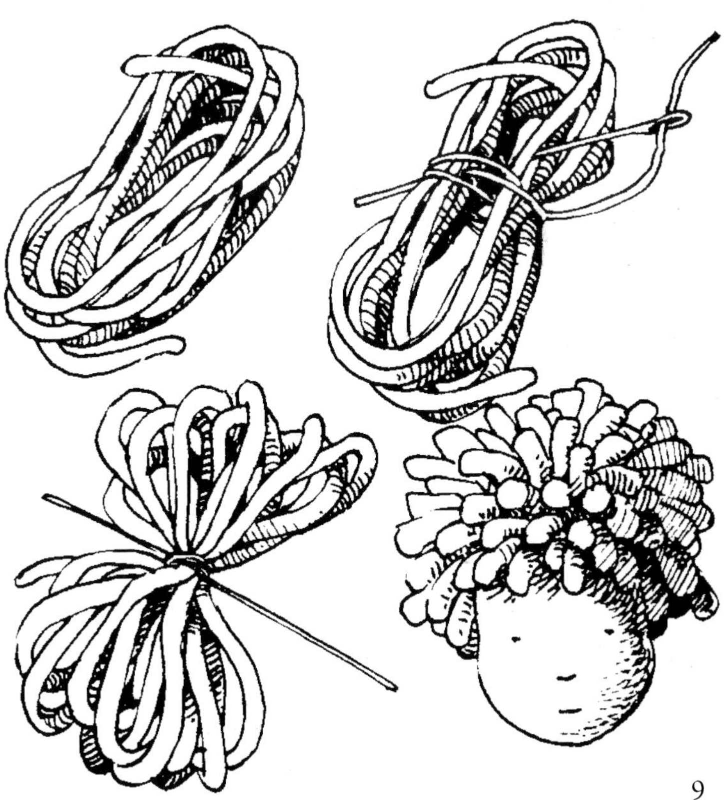

# Wooden Standing Dolls

You can buy wooden dolls in many shapes and sizes, either with a cylindrical body or with one which widens out towards the bottom. The larger wooden dolls sometimes have a hole in the base so that they can be used as finger puppets.

When you buy the dolls, check carefully that the heads are smooth and round and that they are not pitted.

If you are unable to buy a wooden doll you can make one out of a cork and a large wooden bead.

Pare the top of the cork to make a round sloping side (Figure 3).

Make a hole in the top of the cork with a wooden skewer or cocktail stick. Cover the end of the skewer with glue and stick it firmly into the hole.

Then glue a large wooden bead on to the skewer. Cut off the remainder of the skewer.

To finish, wrap a thick thread around the neck, leaving a neck of roughly 1/4 in (5 mm) (Figure 3).

3 *Wooden dolls*

4 *Wooden gnomes*

## *Gnomes*

*MATERIALS*

- Wooden dolls 2 1/4 in and 3 in (6 and 7 cm) high
- Pieces of felt
- Unspun wool or carded fleece

*METHOD*

Clothe the body by gluing a piece of felt on to it then sew up the back seam. Trim the felt.

The pattern of the jacket in Figure 5 shows the measurements for both the gnomes. Lay the jacket around the body and secure it at the neck with a few stitches.

Before you cut out the cap pattern in Figure 5, check the exact circumference of the head as this can vary.

Cut out the cap from a double piece of felt, sew up the back seam and glue the cap on to the wooden head.

Now take a little tuft of unspun wool or carded fleece and tease it well out before gluing it on to the head as hair and beard.

If you want, you can draw on a face with a coloured pencil.

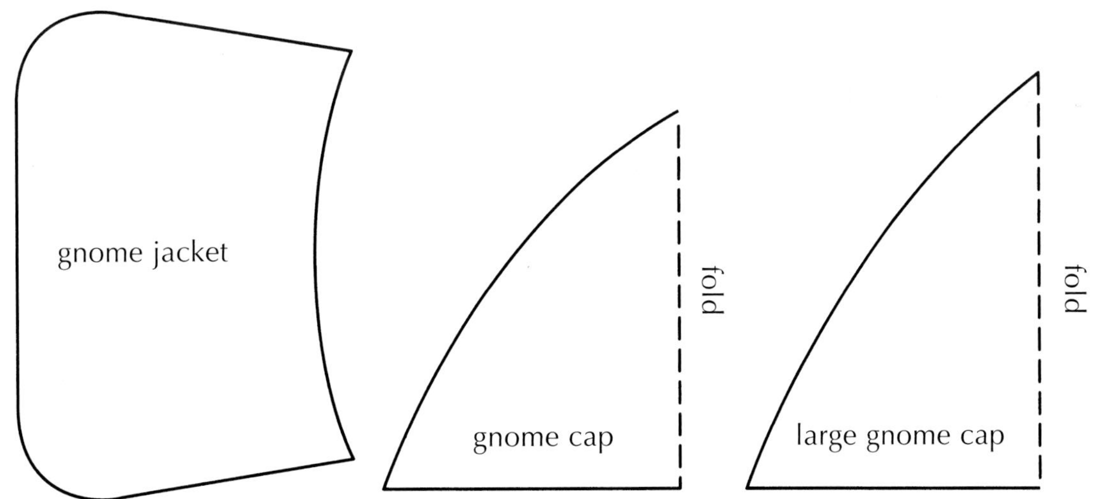


5 *Pattern for wooden gnomes*

## A royal family

MATERIALS

- Wooden dolls, 2 in, 2 1/2 in and 3 in (5, 6 and 7 cm) high
- Pieces of felt
- Unspun wool, carded fleece or knitting wool

METHOD

Clothe the bodies with a felt robe as was described for the gnomes.

Figure 6 shows that the king's robe is embroidered while the queen's is embellished with little beads. Take the measurements of the clothes, cut them out and embroider them before gluing the felt on to the body and sewing it up the back.

### Cloak and jackets

Figure 7 shows the patterns for the king's cloak and the jackets for the rest of the family. Each one is differently made and embroidered. The princess's coat is 3 1/4 in x 1 1/4 in (8 x 3.2 cm). Cut out the edges with pinking shears.

Cut out each item of clothing and embroider it. Gather the top edge and secure it around the doll's neck.

### Finishing off

Make the dolls' hair and the king's white beard from unspun wool or carded fleece (see page 7) and glue them on. The princess has a plait of yellow teased fleece (or thick knitting wool).

Gather the top edge of the queen's veil, then glue it to the back of her head. Finally cut out the crowns and stitch them to the hair.

6 A royal family

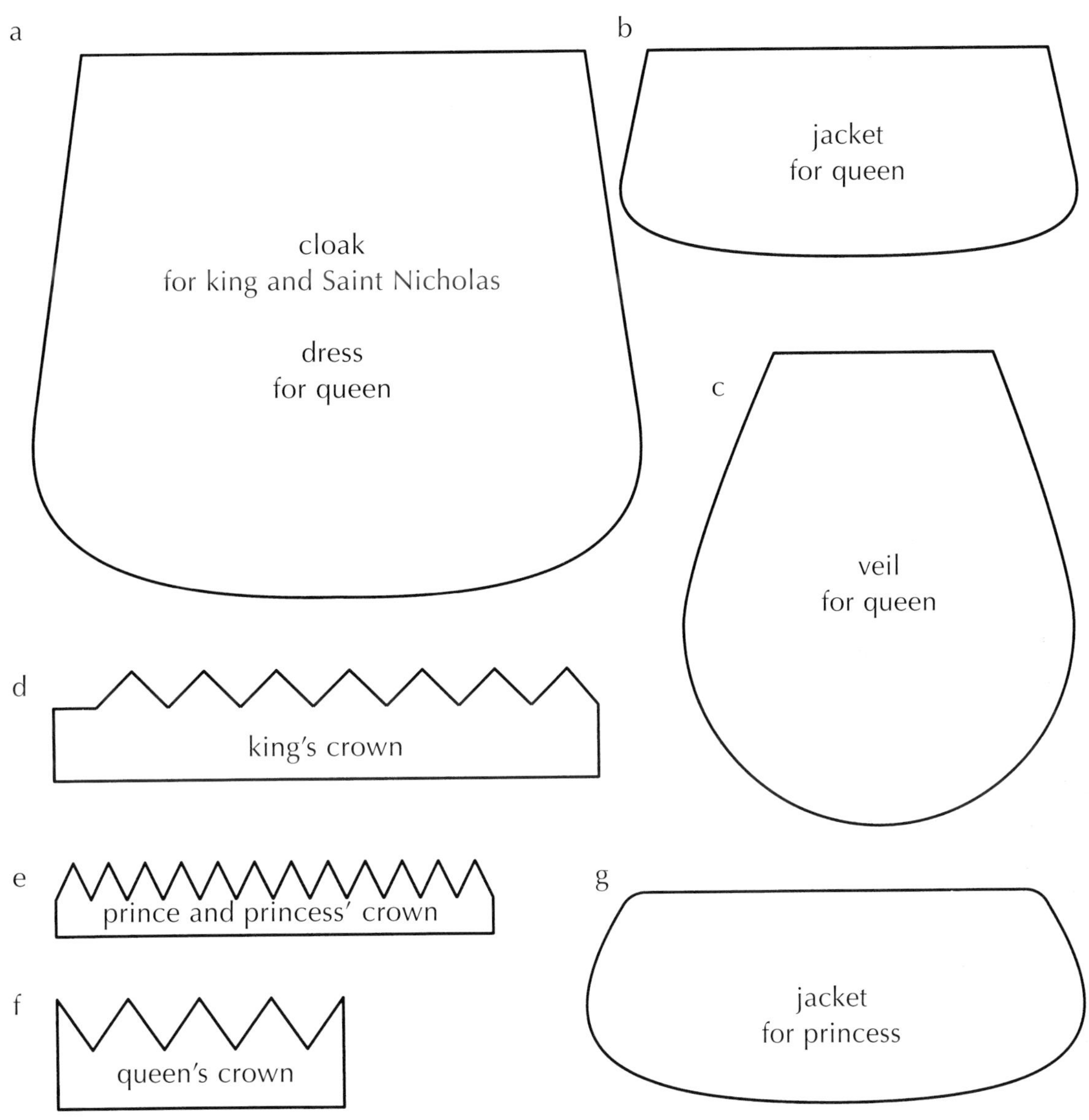


*7 Pattern for the royal family*

## *Saint Nicholas*

*MATERIALS*

- Wooden dolls 2 3/4 in and 2 in (7 and 5 cm) high
- Pieces of felt and a scrap of lace
- Unspun wool or carded fleece
- Stiff card

*METHOD*

Make St Nicholas in the same way as the king (see the pattern in Figure 7). His robe is about 1/2 in (1 cm) shorter and has a lace bottomed hem. Glue a red strip of felt behind the lace. When you sew on the gold trimmings, remember that the inside of the cloak is visible so you must not let the stitches go right through the felt (Figure 8).

St Nicholas has an embroidered mitre (see pattern in Figure 9a). Cut the staff out of felt and card. Glue the card on to the back of the felt.

*Peter*

In the Netherlands Saint Nicholas has one or more companions called Peter. Here is a pattern for a large Peter and a small one (Figure 8).

Blacken the wooden dolls' heads with poster paint or Indian ink. For the clothes, make tubes out of the pieces of felt. For the big Peter you will need a piece of felt about 3 1/2 in x 1 1/2 in (9 x 4 cm); and for the little Peter 2 3/4 in x 1 1/4 in (7 x 3.5 cm). In both cases, gather the tube in at the top and secure it around the neck. The clothes are not glued to the wooden bodies.

Cut out the collar, gather it in at the top and secure it to the neck in the same way.

Each Peter has a different head-covering. For the big Peter gather the cap along the edge, draw it in around the head and secure. Little Peter has a Tyrolean hat: cut out a round piece of felt, gather it along the edge and draw the thread in to the circumference of the head.

8 *Saint Nicholas and Peter*

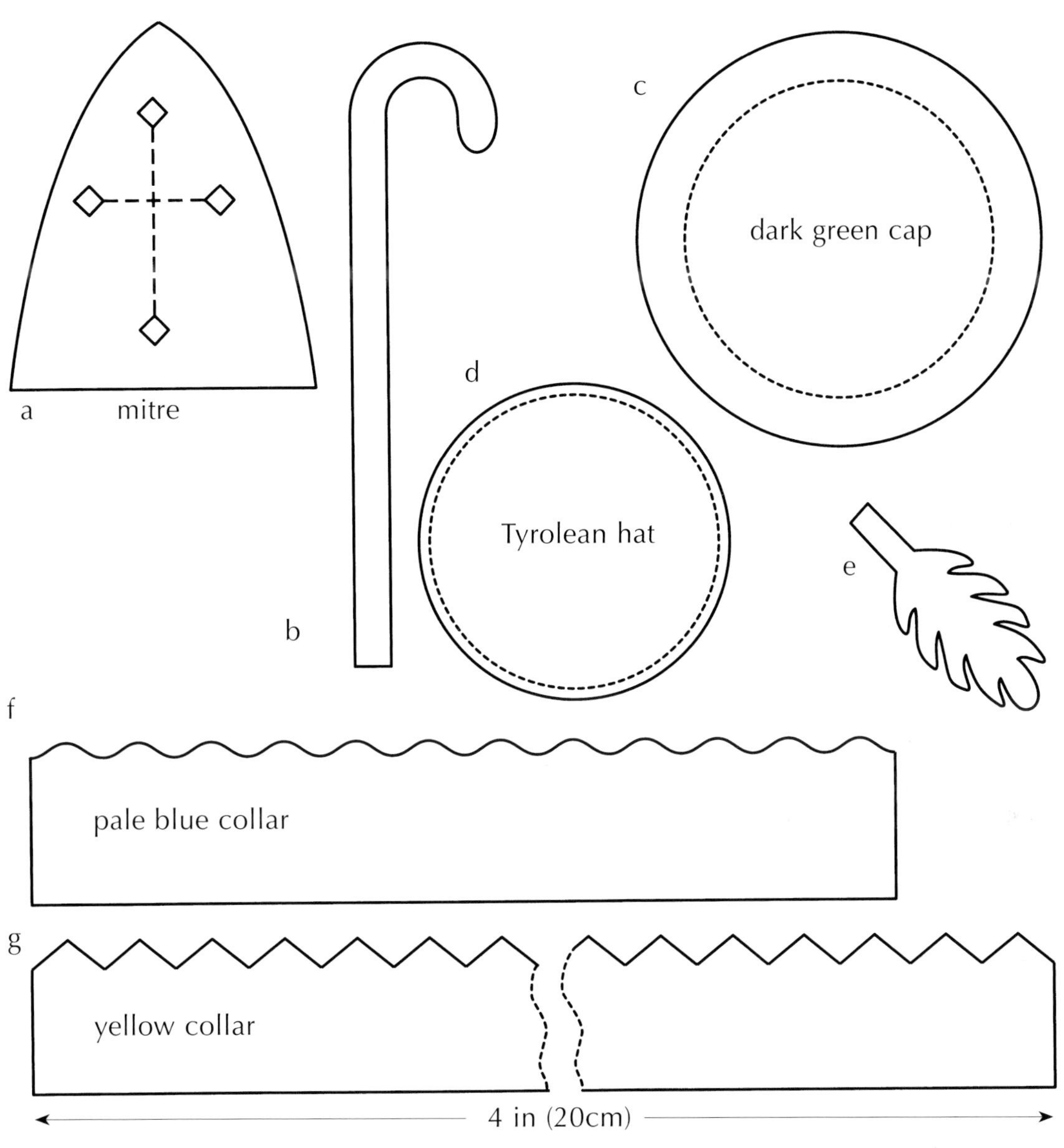


9 *Pattern for Saint Nicholas and Peter*

## Little angel

*MATERIALS*

- Wooden doll 2 3/4 in (7 cm) high
- Pieces of felt
- Little beads
- Carded fleece
- Gold foil

*METHOD*

Clothe the body with a piece of white felt.

Trim the bottom of the angel's dress with a thin strip of felt or some beads.

Cut out the wings (Figure 10). Decorate them either with little beads or with different coloured pieces of felt with matching designs cut into them (Figure 11). These pieces can be glued on to the wings.

Use teased wool for the hair. You can give the angel a hairband and a little star.

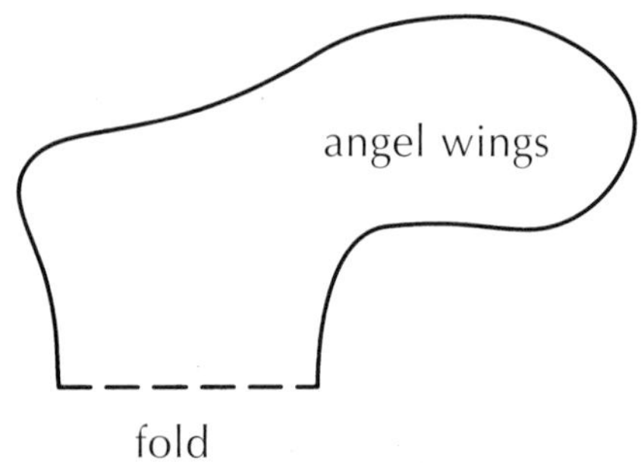


10

11 *Angels*

12 *Mother with baby*

## *Mother with baby*

*MATERIALS*

- Wooden dolls 2 1/4 in and 1 1/4 in (6 and 3 cm) in length
- Pieces of felt
- Pipe-cleaners
- Unvarnished wooden beads about 1/4 in (7 mm) diameter
- Walnut shells

*The mother*

Glue a piece of felt on to the larger wooden doll's body. Sew up the back seam and trim the felt.

Take a piece of pipe-cleaner about 2 1/2 in (6–7 cm) long and stick beads on to each end to make hands.

Then cut out the coat (Figure 13a) and drape it around the doll's neck so that the opening is at the back. Lay the doll face down and put the pipe-cleaner arms over its back. Then sew up the back seam of the coat, thus securing the arms.

Now cut out the headscarf (Figure 13b) and embroider the front with a woollen or cotton thread. Gather in the two bottom edges of the headscarf and glue on to the head.

*The baby*

Glue a little piece of felt around the body and a strip of felt around the neck for a collar. Cut out the cap (Figure 13d), glue it on to the head and secure with a few stitches. If you wish, you can give the baby some hair with some strands of wool.

*The cradle*

Cut out the sleeping bag (Figure 13c), lay the baby on the wide half, and fold the narrow half back over the body. Bring the sides up around the baby and sew up the side seams. Take the baby out of the sleeping bag and glue the bottom of the bag into the inside of half a walnut shell. Make sure you can still slip the baby in and out easily.

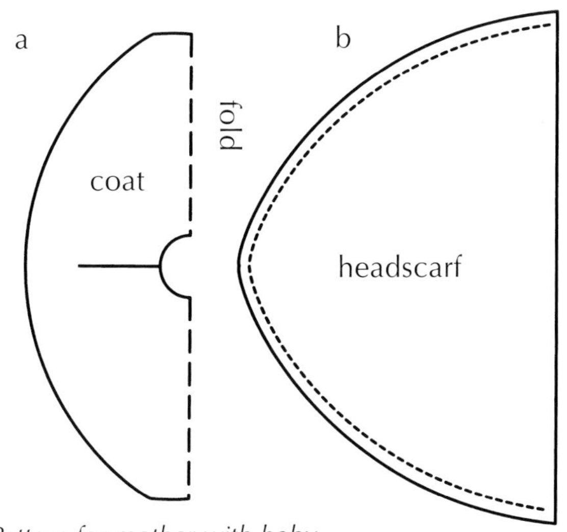


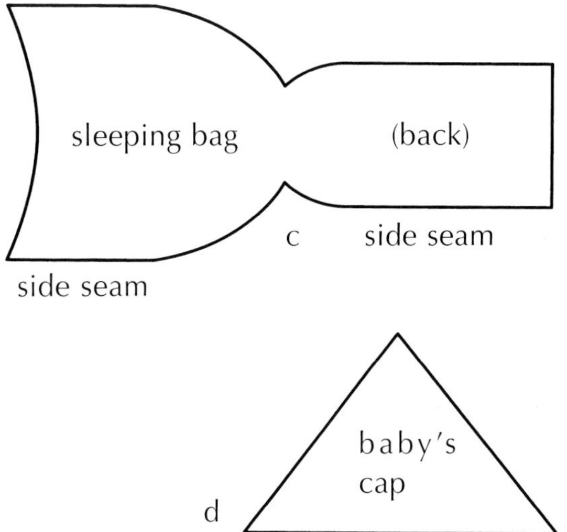


13 *Pattern for mother with baby*

## *Hazelnut children*

*MATERIALS*

- Hazelnuts
- Unvarnished wooden beads with a diameter of 1/2–5/8 in (12–15 mm)
- Pieces of felt
- Unspun wool

*METHOD*

Wipe the hazelnuts clean and if necessary scrape the bottoms flat so that the children will not fall over. Glue a bead on to the top of each hazelnut for a head. Make sure the hole in the bead runs from top to bottom.

Take a tiny bit of unspun wool or some woollen yarn for the hair and glue this on to the head.

Cut out a piece of felt 1 in (2.5 cm) wide and 2 in (5 cm) long (depending on the size of the bead) and glue it to the head as a headscarf or bonnet. Tie it at the neck with a piece of yarn (Figure 14).

First trim the bottom of the felt and then glue it securely on to the hazelnut. If you wish, you can draw on eyes and mouth with a coloured pencil.

14 *Hazlenut children*

# Felt Dolls

## Basic model

*MATERIALS*

- White, pink or brown cotton knit
- Unspun wool
- Pieces of felt
- Thread
- Thin card

### *The head*

Take a piece of cotton knit about 3 x 3 in (8 x 8 cm). Make a little ball from unspun wool, about 3/4 in (2 cm) in diameter, and lay it in the middle of the cotton. Wrap the cotton round the ball of wool and tie it around the neck (Figure 15b).

Make sure that the head has as few creases as possible on one side, and use this side for the face. Trim the excess cotton straight across about 1 in (2.5 cm) under the tie.

Later, once the doll is finished, you can carefully embroider the face. In order to get the eyes and mouth in the right place, stick pins with coloured heads into the right places first.

### *The body*

For the body of, for example, the flower children (page 23) and the finger puppets (page 29) you will need a tube of felt. Vary the length and width of the body according to the doll.

Take a square piece of felt and sew two opposite sides together as shown in Figure 15c. Now gather in one of the open ends to make a neck. Insert the head into this gathered end of the tube, draw in the thread and sew the neck firmly into the tube (Figure 15d).

The doll should now be able to stand, but if you stuff the tube with wool it will be firmer. You can also sew a round piece of felt of the same colour across the base. The doll will stand better if you cut out a round piece of cardboard and stick it on to the felt base. Make the cardboard roughly 1/16 in (2 mm) smaller than the felt base.

Now the basic form of the doll is finished.

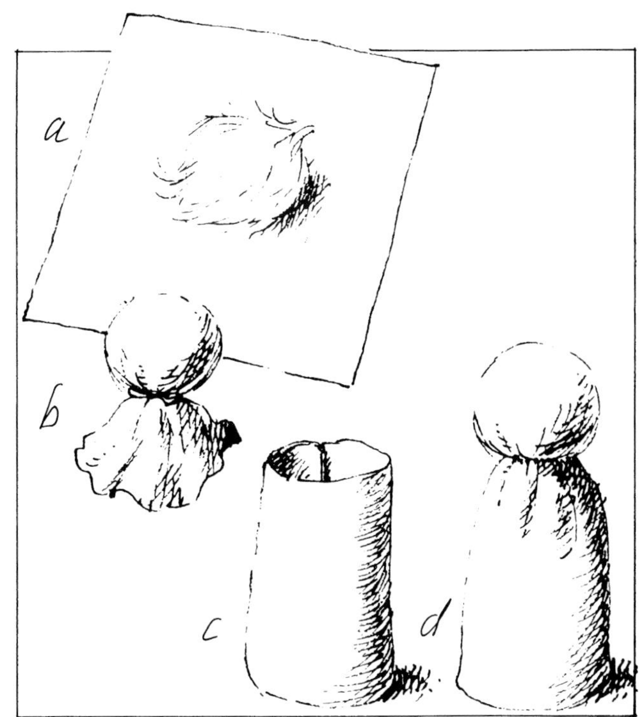


15 *Pattern for basic doll*

16 *Gnomes*

## *Gnomes*

*MATERIALS*

- Pieces of felt
- Unspun wool or carded fleece

*METHOD*

Cut out the gnome's coat (Figure 17). Sew up the seam of the hood and run a gathering thread through at the place marked 'gather.' Stuff a tuft of well-teased wool into the coat, draw in the thread and either tie it firmly at the front or sew up the coat. To make a beard, draw out a little bit of the wool from the head or sew on a bit of wool. You can also tease out wool around the face.

Trim the wool at the bottom to make a flat base so that the gnome can stand. Using the same proportions but changing the lengths shown in the pattern, you will be able to make different sized standing gnomes. Make sure that the heads do not become too small.

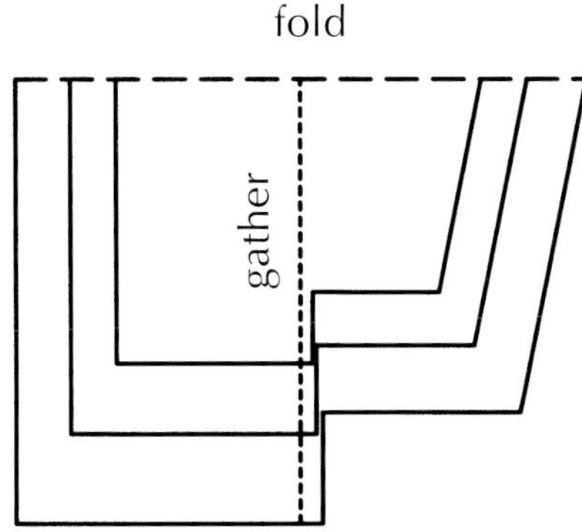


17 *Pattern for gnome's coat*

## *Woollen dolls*

*MATERIALS*

- Thick knitting wool in different colours
- Sewing thread in the same colours as the wool
- Sewing thread in contrasting colours
- Stiff card

*METHOD*

The dolls shown in Figure 20 vary in length between 2 1/4 and 3 1/4 in (6 and 8 cm). For the arms, wind the knitting wool around a piece of card about 2 1/2 in (6 cm) long (the width is not important). Depending on the thickness of the wool, about twenty turns should do.

Tie up the ends with some thread of the same colour (Figure 18b). These will eventually be little round hands. Take the wool right off the card and tie it up at the wrists, about 1/2 in (1 cm) from the ends (Figure 18c).

The head and the body are made using one piece of card. Take a piece of card about 2 3/4 in (7 cm) long and wind the knitting wool around it about forty times, again depending on the thickness of the wool. Tie up one end of the yarn, where the head will be, and take the wool off the card. Now tie up the head at the neck about 3/4 in (2 cm) from the top (Figure 19a).

Now thrust the arms through the loop of the chest and then tie in the waist (Figure 19b).

Pull the waist up a bit so that the arms sit tight. You can also secure the arms more firmly by criss-crossing the thread over the chest.

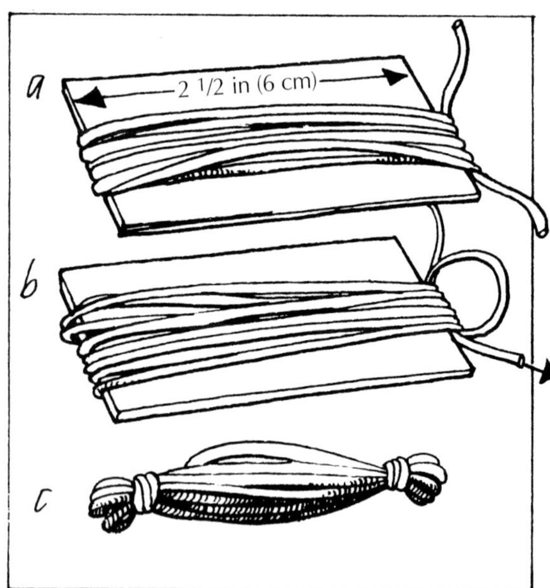


18

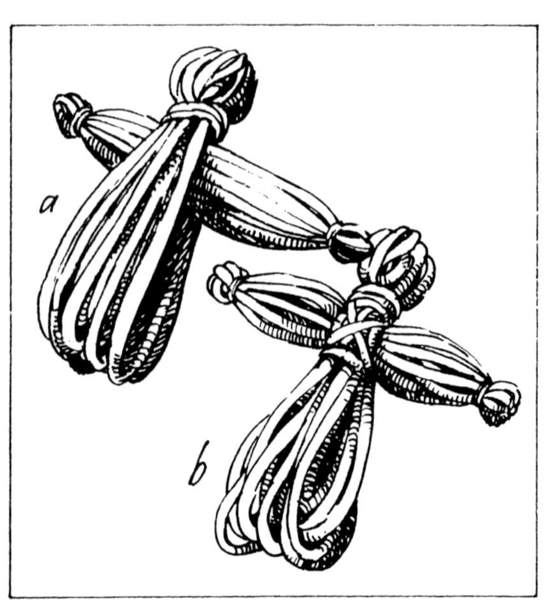


19

To make a doll with a skirt, cut open the loops at the bottom.

To make legs, divide the loops into two equal parts and finish off as for the hands.

You can dress the dolls by giving them a conical cap made of felt, a belt, a scarf or an apron.

If you wish, you can cut open the hands and feet like the first doll in Figure 20. This makes a kind of brush effect.

20 *Woollen dolls*

## *Flower children*

*MATERIALS*

- Pieces of felt
- Pink or white cotton knit
- Unspun wool
- Carded wool or magic wool
- Pipe-cleaners
- Sewing thread

*GENERAL METHOD*

For the head, see the description on page 19. Vary the length and width of the body according to the kind of flower child.

The doll will stand as it is, but you can also fill the tube with wool and sew a round piece of felt of the same colour across the base, first sticking a round piece of card on to the bottom of the base. The card should be 1/16 in (2 mm) smaller than the round piece of felt. Flower children that carry flowers are inclined to topple over, so it is a good idea to sew in a marble or a pebble as a stabilizing weight.

This completes the basic construction of the flower children. The details for each specific flower follow.

*The crocus*

For the body take a piece of felt 2 1/4 x 2 1/4 in (6 x 6 cm). For the collar take a piece of lilac-coloured felt 4 x 1 1/2 in (10 x 3.5 cm), and cut it out as in Figure 21a. Gather in the top edge and sew the collar around the neck.

Do the same for the crocus's cap. Gather the felt in a little at the place indicated so that the cap sits neatly on the head, but first give the flower child some hair of a suitable colour (using magic wool for example). Secure the cap on to the head with a few stitches and then secure the tops of the petals, drawing together the ones which lie opposite each other.

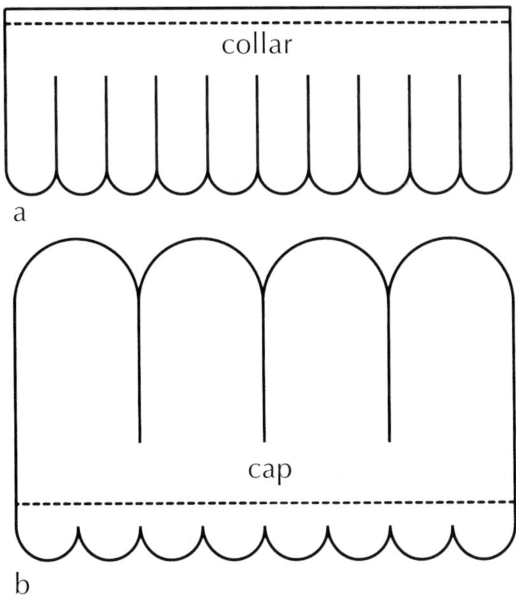


21 *Pattern for crocus*

22 *Flower children*

*The snowdrop*

The snowdrop's body is 2 1/4 in (6 cm) high and 2 3/4 in (7 cm) wide. Cut out the collar (Figure 23a), gather it in and sew it on to the body.

The snowdrop's bonnet consists of three separate white petals (Figure 23b) sewn on to the top of a light-green felt stalk (Figure 23c). First give the flower child's head some white woollen hair, then sew on the bonnet with a few stitches.

The snowdrop holds a separate flower which consists of a green stalk with three separate white petals (Figure 24d). The piece of felt for the stalk is 5 x 1/2 in (12 1/2 x 1 1/2 cm) rolled lengthwise around a pipe-cleaner and secured to it. The petals can then be sewn on.

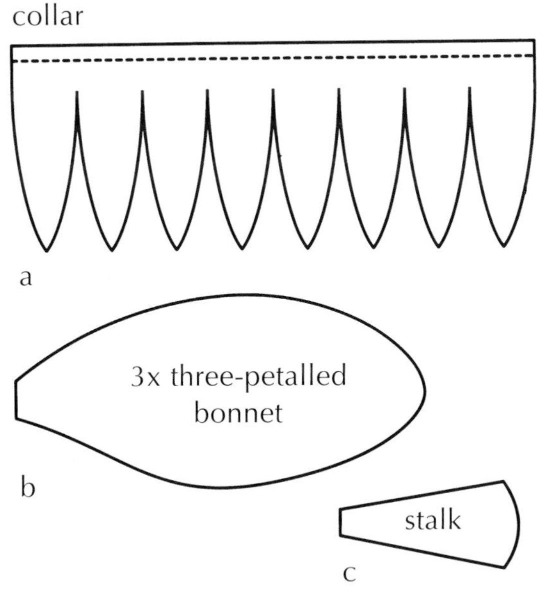


23 Pattern for snowdrop

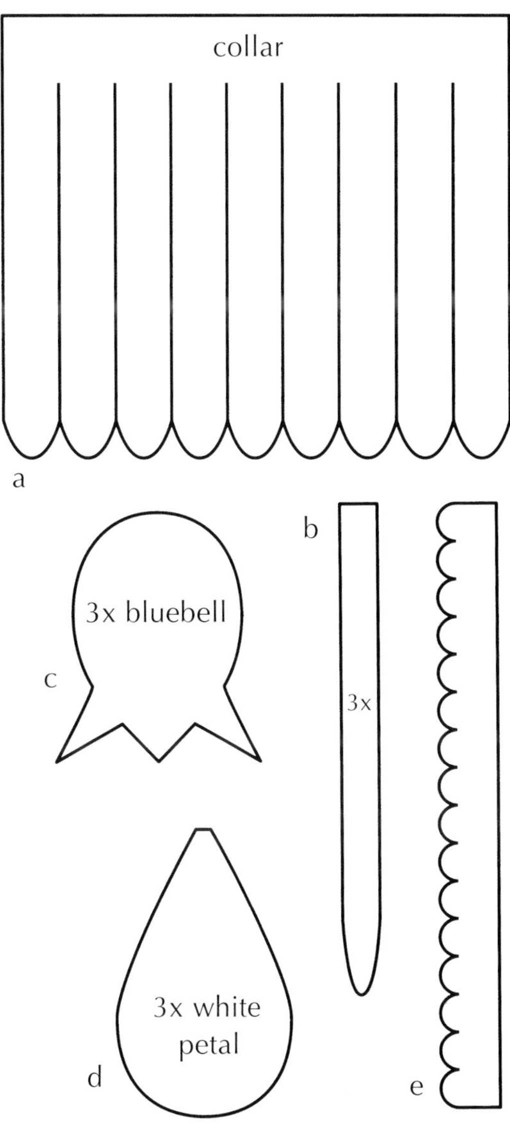


24 Pattern for bluebell and snowdrop

*The bluebell*

The bluebell's body is 2 3/4 in (7 cm) high and 2 1/4 in (6 cm) wide. Cut out the collar (Figure 24a), gather it in and sew it on to the neck.

The bluebell wears a petal hairband of blue felt (Figures 22 and 24e). To make the stalk for the separate flower, follow the same procedure as described for the snowdrop. The bluebell then has three extra petals (Figure 24c) which must be sewn together and then secured to the stalk.

*The tulip*

The tulip's body is 2 1/4 in (5.5 cm) high and 4 in (10 cm) wide. Cut out the collar (Figure 25a), gather it in and sew it on to the body.

The tulip child has a bonnet of six separate petals (Figure 25b). Sew the first two petals on to the side of the head. Then gather the remaining four petals in a little at the bottom, before sewing them on to the head overlapping each other (Figure 25c). Give the tulip some pink coloured hair.

*The daffodil*

The daffodil's body is about 2 in (5 cm) high and 4 in (10 cm) wide. Cut out the collar (Figure 26a), gather it and sew it on to the body.

The daffodil's bonnet consists of two parts. First sew the gathered yellow wreath of petals on to the head. Next cut out a circle of dark yellow felt to make the heart of the flower. Make cuts into the opposite sides of the circle as in Figure 26c and sew up the inside as in the drawing so that it stands up as a dome. Sew the heart on to the crown of the head.

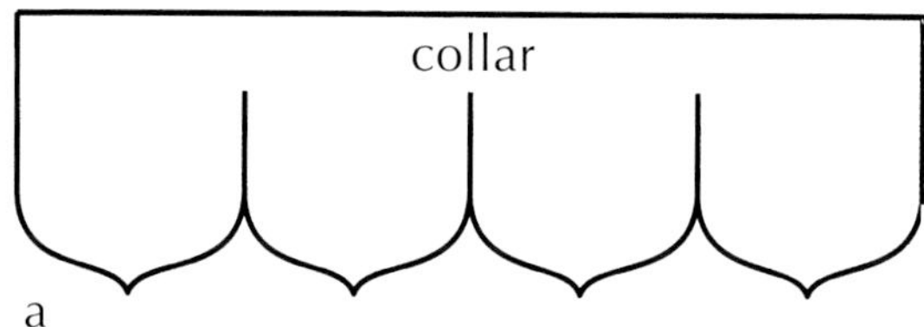


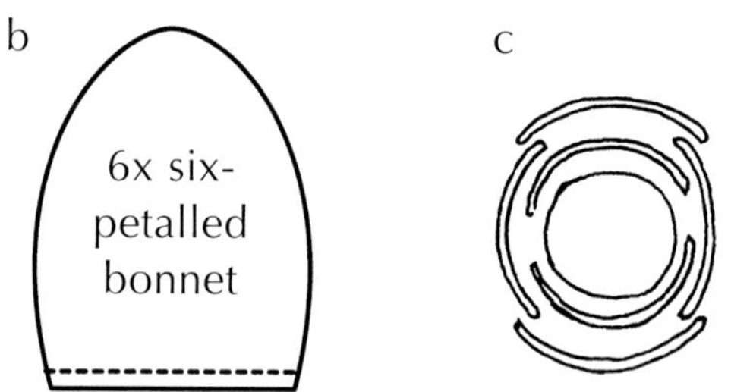


25 *Pattern for tulip*

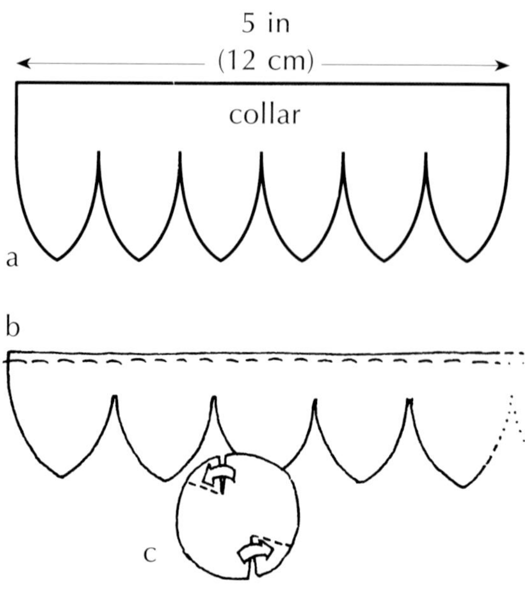


26 *Pattern for daffodil*

## *Blossom fairies*

*MATERIALS*

- Pieces of felt
- Pink cotton knit
- Unspun wool
- Carded fleece in various colours
- Two unvarnished wooden beads, diameter 1/4 in (5 mm)
- Length of pipe-cleaner
- Piece of thin card
- Glue

*METHOD*

Follow the description on page 19 for the head.

Now make the gown. Choose soft colours to match the blossoms: white, pink, pale yellow and pale green.

Fold the piece of felt in half and cut out the pattern in Figure 29. Open the gown and cut the opening for the neck.

Push the head through the opening in the gown. Sew up the back seam of the neck-opening and secure the neck firmly to the gown (Figure 28).

27 *Blossom fairies*

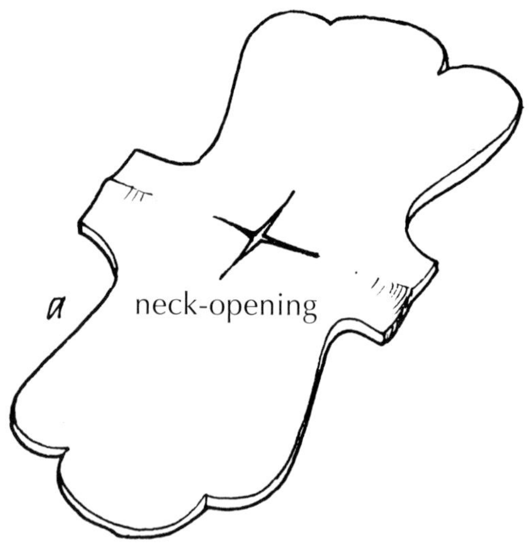


To make the arms take about 3 1/4 in (8 cm) of pipe-cleaner and insert it into the open sleeves of the gown. Now sew up the sleeves to secure the pipe-cleaner, which should now stick out from the sleeves. Apply a little glue to the ends of the pipe-cleaner and fix on the beads. As soon as the glue is dry, any surplus pipe-cleaner can be cut off.

Tease out a little bit of carded fleece or unspun wool and sew it firmly on to the head, together with a felt hairband.

You can also fix a thread on to the top of the head to hang up the blossom fairy. Do not use too short a thread: it can always be shortened afterwards. Hang the blossom fairy among attractive branches (Figure 27).

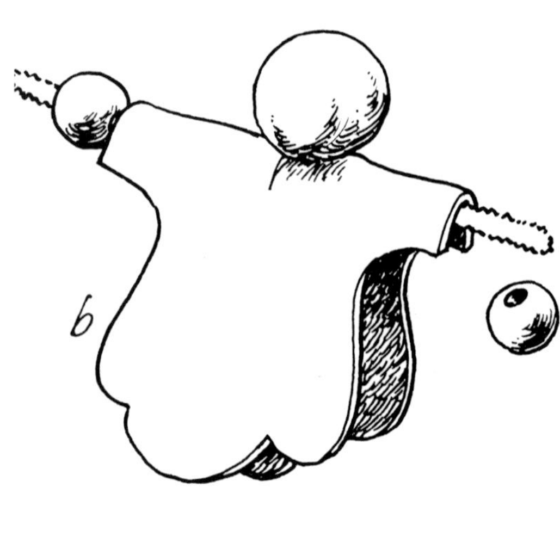


28

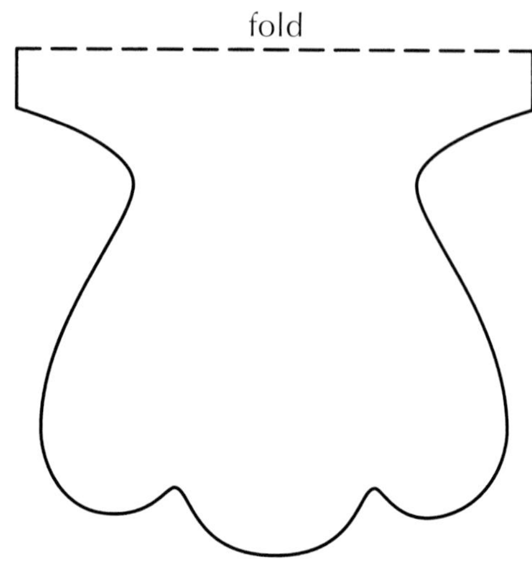


29 *Pattern for blossom fairy*

## *Finger puppets*

*MATERIALS*

- Pieces of felt
- Unspun wool
- Cotton knit in various colours
- Darning wool in various colours
- Beads with a diameter or 1 1/4 in (32 mm)
- Small beads

*METHOD*

Finger puppets must not only be able to stand, they must also fit on to fingers, so that they can act out stories. Children love to play with them.

The total height of these finger puppets is about 3 1/4 in (8 cm); the head has a diameter of about 3/4 in (2 cm).

Follow the description on page 19 for the head. Make the body from a rectangular piece of felt 3 x 2 1/4 in (7.5 x 6 cm). Sew the back seams together to make a tube (Figure 15c on page 19) Gather in the neck as shown, insert the head and secure it.

### *Dressing the finger puppets*

Figure 31 shows how the finger puppets can be dressed differently. You may wish to invent your own variations.

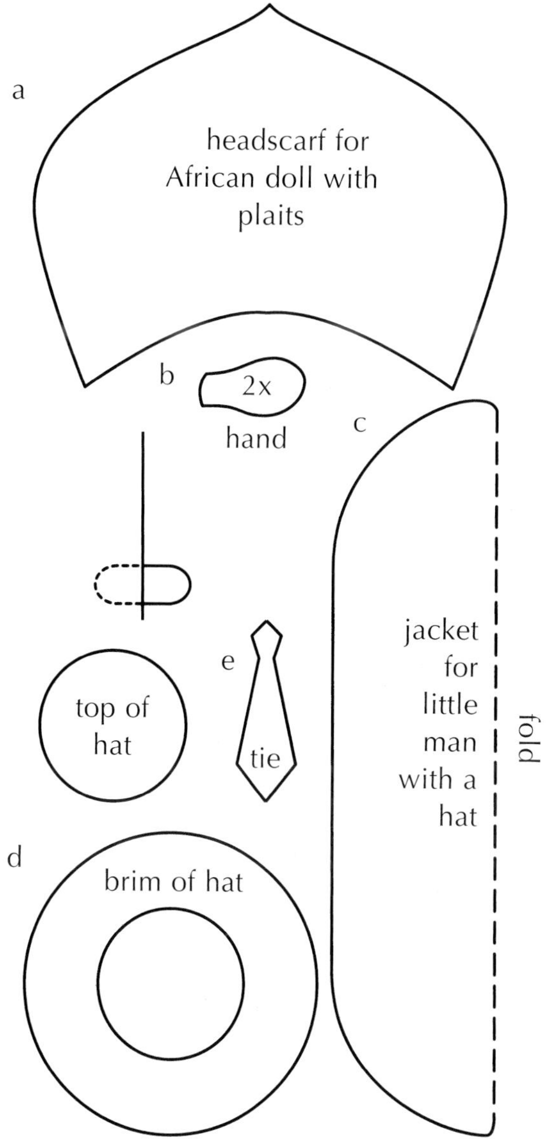


30 *Pattern for finger puppets*

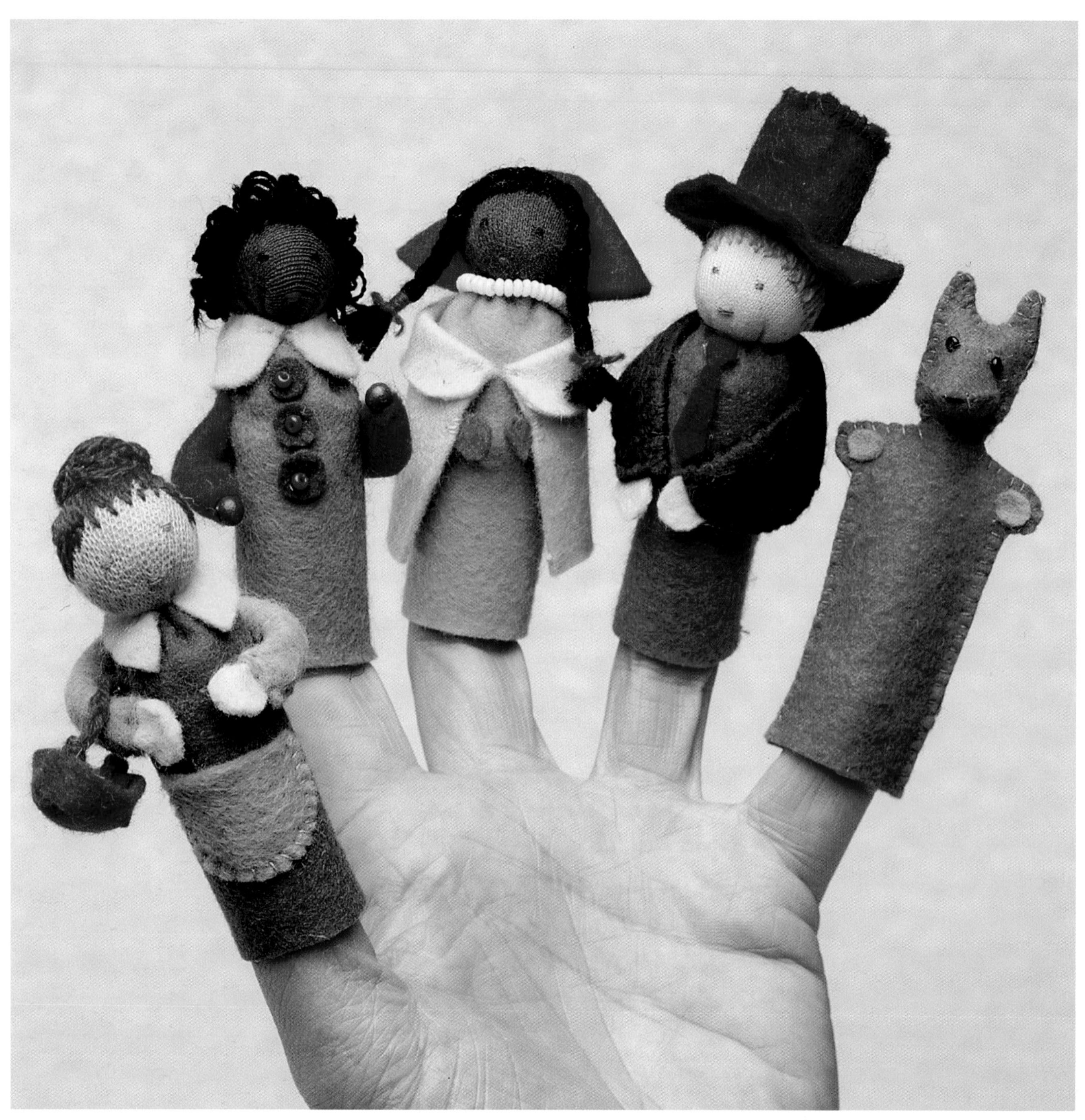

31 *Finger puppets*

*African doll with plaits*

Take a piece of felt 3 1/2 x 2 1/4 in (9 x 5.5 cm) for the coat. Fold over 1/2 in (1 cm) of the top of the coat to make a collar. Trim around the corners. Sew the hands on to the coat (Figure 31). Place the coat firmly around the doll's neck and sew it on securely a bit lower down at the front.

Secure the headscarf (Figure 30a) on to the head around the face, with the point at the back sewn on to the doll's back.

Make the plaits out of black darning wool. Tie the ends together and sew them on to the headscarf on the head. Embroider a fringe over the forehead. Give the doll a necklace of beads.

*Little man with a hat*

This doll wears a jacket which consists of two large sleeves only. Two hands are sewn on to these. The top edge of the sleeves is sewn on to the tube body along the whole length, from one wrist to the other.

Cut out the tie (Figure 30e) and secure it with a few stitches. Use light-coloured darning wool to embroider hair from the crown of the head downwards.

The hat consists of three parts: a piece of felt 2 1/2 x 1 in (6.5 x 2.5 cm) and the two round pieces (Figure 30d). Cut out the parts of the hat, sew them together and secure them to the head.

*Woman with a bun*

This woman has an apron sewn on to her body. For the arms take a piece of felt 3 1/2 x 3/4 in (9 x 2 cm). Fold the piece in half to 3 1/2 x 3/8 in (9 x 1 cm), insert a pipe-cleaner into it and sew up the long seam. Then secure the hands in the sleeves and fasten the arms on to the back of

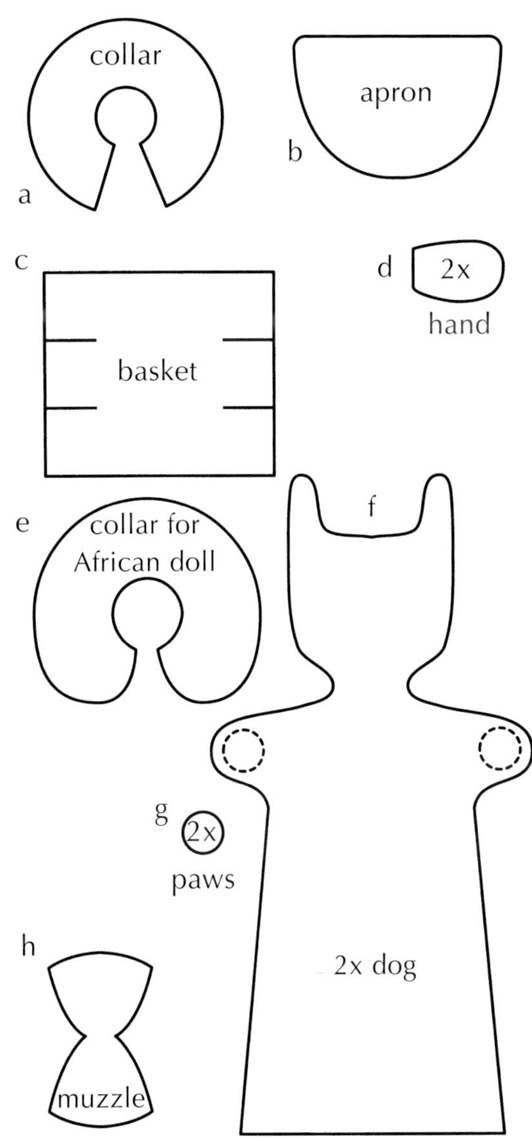


32 *Patterns for finger puppets*

the tube body. Cut out the collar and sew it on (patterns are in Figures 32a–d).

Embroider the hair from the crown of the head downwards.

For the bun, twist a length of woollen yarn around your finger thirty or forty times (depending on the thickness of the wool). Remove the wool from your finger, twist it into a bun and secure it to the back of the head with a few large stitches. Finally make the basket for her to hold.

### *African doll*

This doll is made in a similar way to the woman with a bun but with this one the collar is quite a bit bigger (Figure 32e), there are big buttons on the dress and the hands are beads sewn on to the sleeves.

Make the hair by embroidering large loops, taking the needle back through the loop each time to secure it.

### *Little dog*

The pattern of the little dog has an identical front and back, and a separate muzzle.

Cut out the pattern of Figure 32f and sew the two pieces together, filling the head with wool.

Now sew the muzzle together, stuff it with wool and sew it on to the front of the head.

Finish off the dog by giving him two beads for eyes and sewing two little circles on to his paws (Figure 32g). Embroider the mouth on the muzzle.

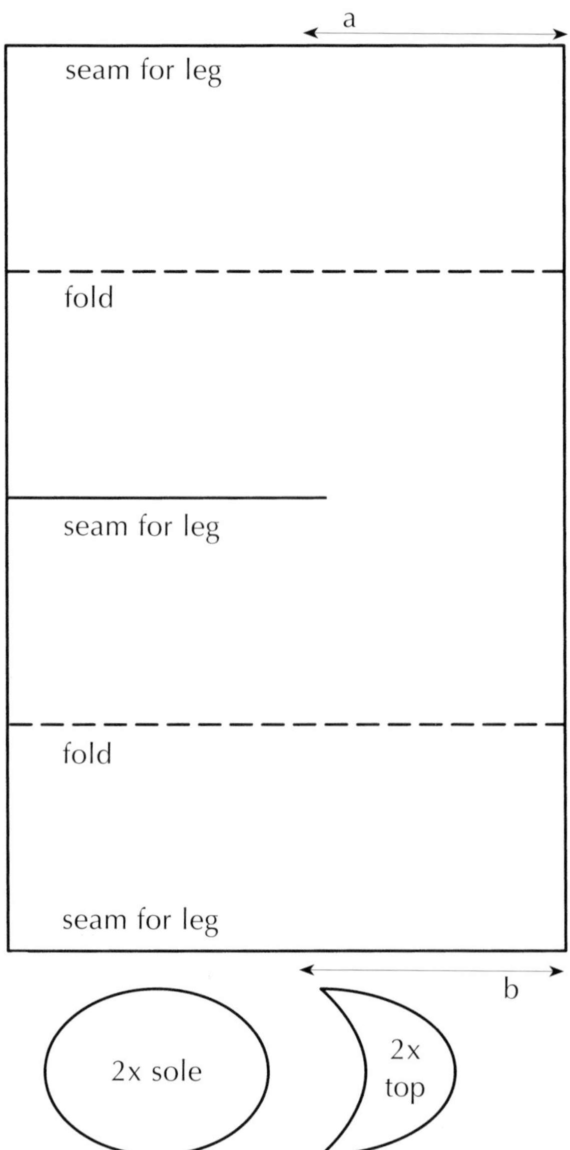


33 *Pattern for walking dolls*

## *Walking dolls*

*MATERIALS*

- Pieces of felt
- Unspun wool
- Cotton knit for the head and hands
- Knitting wool
- Pipe-cleaner

*METHOD*

Make a round head with a diameter of about 1 1/4 in (3 cm) from unspun wool and a piece of cotton knit. See page 19 for method.

As you can see in Figure 34, you can make these dolls walk. They consist of two parts: the upper body and the lower body, the latter being sewn to the former at the back. Both the man and the woman wear trousers; the woman wears hers under her dress.

For the arms and hands take a pipe-cleaner, doubling the two ends back a short way, leaving the length of the pipe-cleaner at about 5 in (12.5 cm). Wrap some teased unspun wool thinly around the pipe-cleaner and tie a piece of cotton knit around both ends to make the hands.

The patterns in Figure 33 are for a pair of trousers with baggy legs and for slippers or boots. Figure 35 has patterns for a dress for the woman, a jacket for the man, a headscarf and a pointed hat.

Cut out the various parts of the pattern. Push the head through the neck-opening into the jacket or dress and sew it up.

Open out the jacket or dress and lay the arms inside it, making sure that the hands stick out.

Sew up the seams of the jacket almost completely but leave a little hole so that you can fill it loosely with wool. Then sew up the hole. This completes the upper body.

Cut out the trousers and sew them up so that side *a* is sewn to side *b*.

The man in Figure 34 has boots (you will need a piece of felt 2 1/2 x 1 1/4 in, (6.2 x 3.2 cm) and the woman has a pair of slippers. The procedure for the two of them is the same. Sew the tops of the man's boots to his trousers. Then sew up the soles and uppers of the boots and the slippers, and stuff the tips of the footwear before sewing them on to the bottom of the trouser legs. Sew the front of the trousers on to the waist underneath the jacket or dress. Leave the top of the trousers open at the back so that you can put two fingers into the trouser legs.

Finish off the dolls by giving them a hat or a headscarf — the man can have hair from teased wool, and the woman long hair from thin yellow knitting wool. If you wish you can embroider the eyes and mouth or draw the face with a pencil.

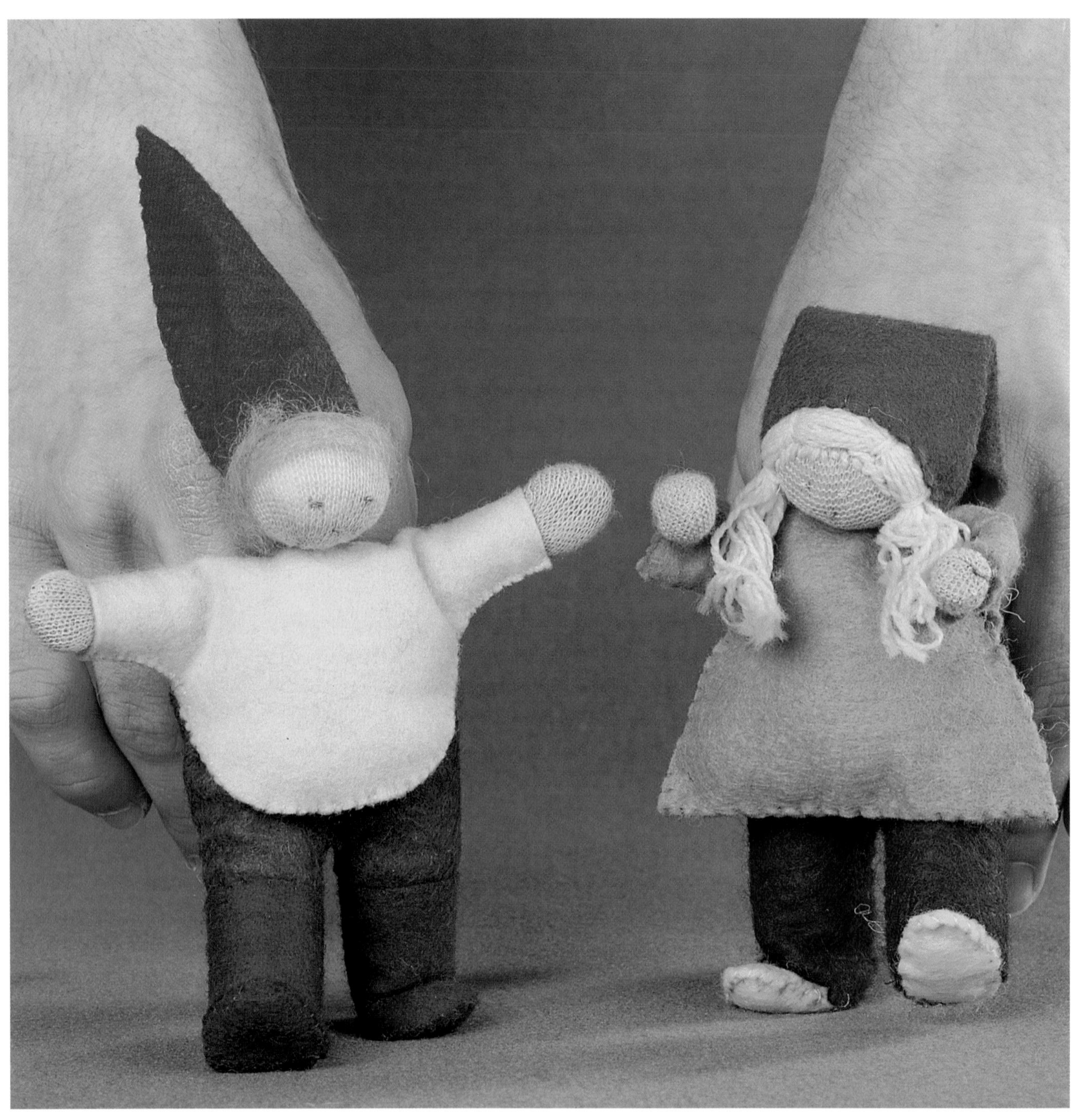

34 *Walking dolls*

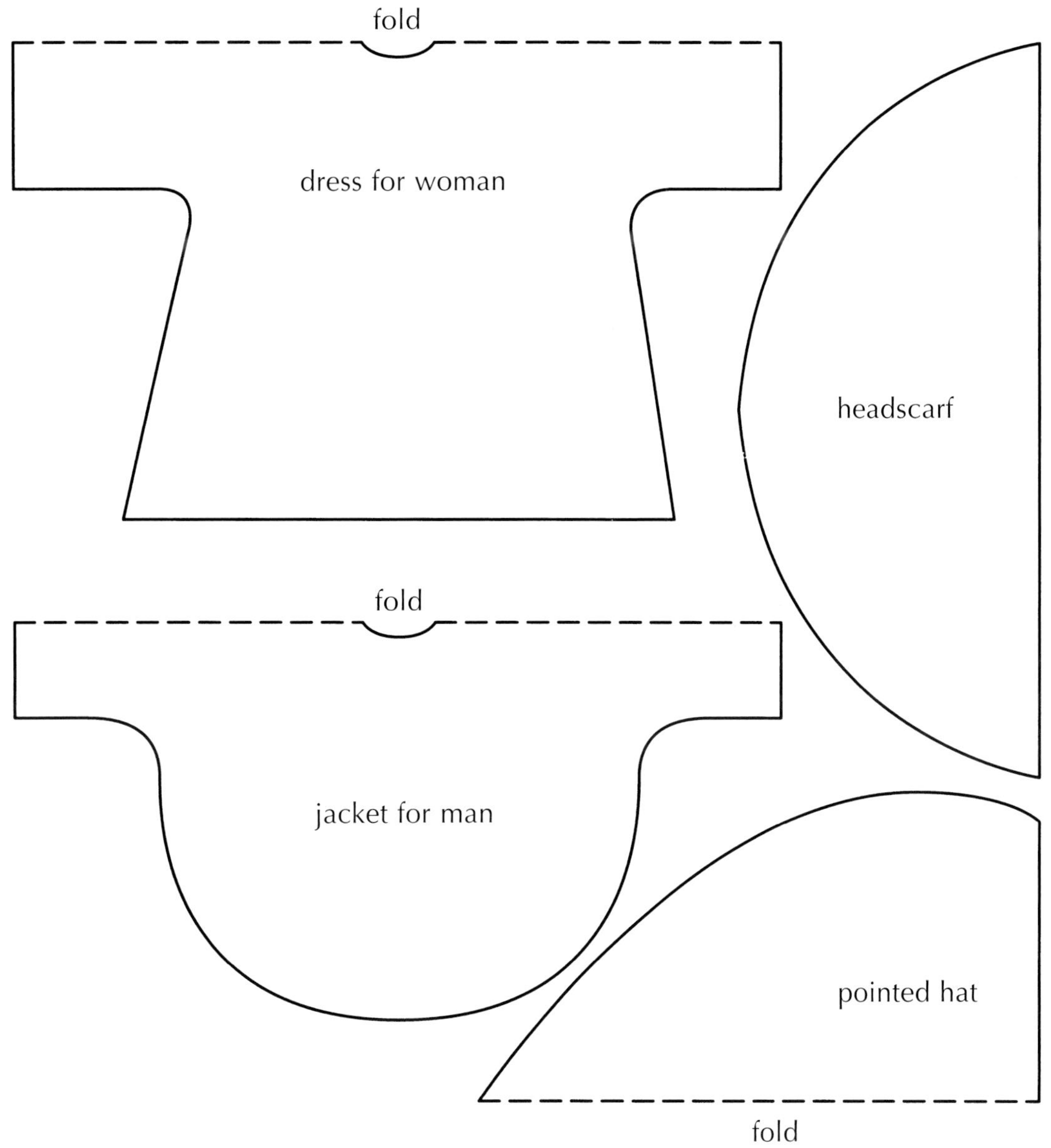
fold
dress for woman
headscarf
fold
jacket for man
pointed hat
fold

35

# Dolls with pipe-cleaner frames

## Basic model

MATERIALS

- Pipe-cleaners
- Unvarnished wooden beads with a diameter of 1/2 x 1/4 in (12 and 5 mm)
- Pieces of felt
- Unspun wool
- Thin yellow wool

METHOD

Double over a pipe-cleaner and glue the folded end into the hole of the 1/2 in (12 mm) bead to make a head (Figure 36a). Now twist a second pipe-cleaner horizontally around the neck of the first to create arms (Figure 36b). Then cut the arms and legs off to the right length.

Now start on the trousers. Cut out the legs from a double piece of felt (Figure 37). The trouser legs should reach up to the armpits. Fold them over the legs and sew them up, securing the top parts together to form the top of the trousers.

Cut out the smock from the pattern in Figure 37 and lay it around the doll's shoulders. Sew up the arms and the back. You can give the doll a different coloured strip of felt around the neck.

Glue unspun wool or some single strands of yarn on to the head for hair.

If you wish, cut out the gnome's cap in Figure 37 and sew it up the back before sticking it to the head.

The dolls are about 2 1/4 in (6 cm) high.

## Girl

The girl in Figure 38 has a dress instead of a smock (see the pattern in Figure 37). Her hair is made from a thin woollen strand. Wind it at least ten times around four fingers. Take it off the fingers and sew these twenty (or so) strands together by taking another strand of wool and threading it through the middle of the hair several times. Then glue the hair on to the head. Once the glue is dry, trim the hair to the correct shape.

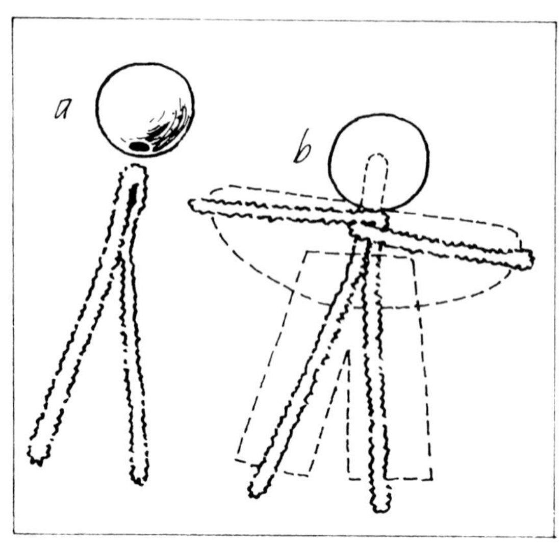


36 Pipe-cleaner frames

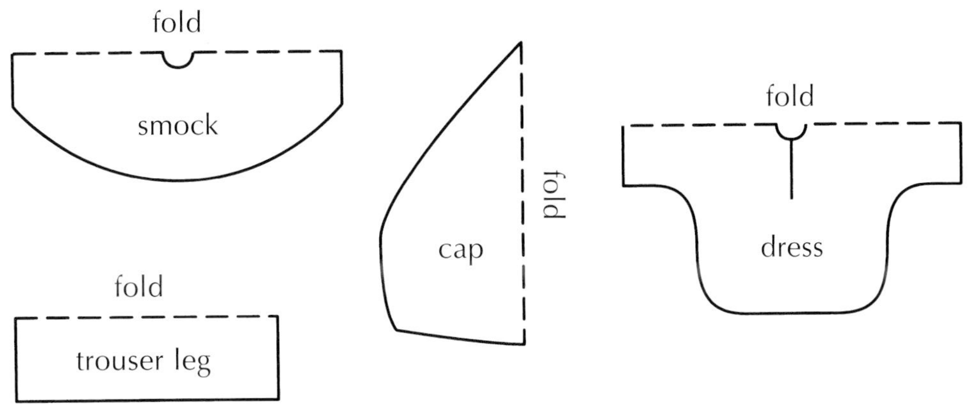


37 *Pattern for dolls' clothes*

38 *Dolls with pipe-cleaner frames*

## *A Christmas gnome*

*MATERIALS*

- A long pipe-cleaner or thin wire
- Plain varnished bead, diameter 1/2 in (12 mm)
- Four red beads, diameter 1/4 in (5 mm)
- Unspun wool or carded fleece
- Pieces of felt
- Glue

*METHOD*

The gnome shown in Figure 39 is about 2 1/4 in (6 cm) tall.

If you do not have pipe-cleaners you can use thin wire to make the frame instead.

Cut off a piece of pipe-cleaner or wire 20–24 in (50–60 cm) long. Push it through the plain varnished bead, which becomes the head. Make sure that the bead is in the middle of the wire with the hole lying vertically. Twist the two ends of the wire together to make a neck of about 1/4 in (5 mm) (Figure 40a).

Now bend the wires out left and right and run a red bead on to each wire. Bend each wire around its bead, bringing the end back to the neck. Twist the wire together, thus making an arm and a hand (length 1 in/2.5cm). The wires now cross at the neck (Figure 40b).

Bring the two wires downwards. Now thread a wire through them 1 1/2 in (4 cm) below the neck to make the legs. Bend the wire back in the same way as for the arms. Finally twist the two leg-wires together up to the armpits. Do this for each leg (Figure 40c).

The frame is now finished. Wrap some thin teased wool or carded fleece around it.

Cut out the pattern in Figure 41 and drape the suit (which is like a boiler-suit) around the doll. Trim if necessary. Sew up the trouser legs and then the arms and finally the back of the suit.

Cut out the cap, sew up the back and glue it to the head. Finally cut out the collar and sew it on.

This gnome can sit on the branch of a Christmas tree. If you wish, you can make it a little bigger.

39 *Christmas gnome*

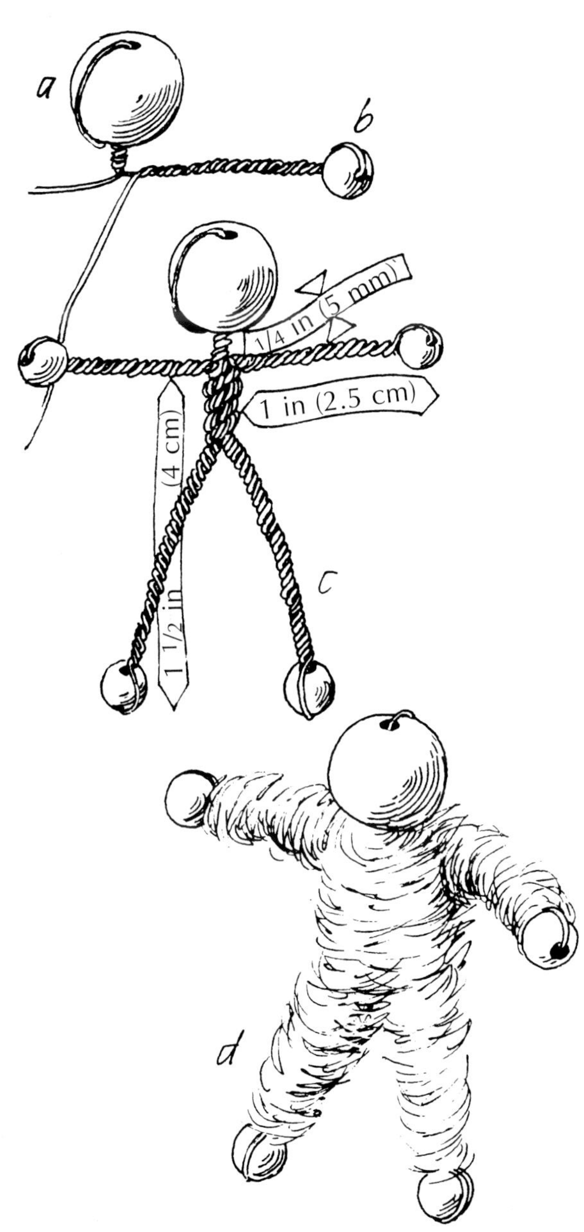


40 *Making the body*

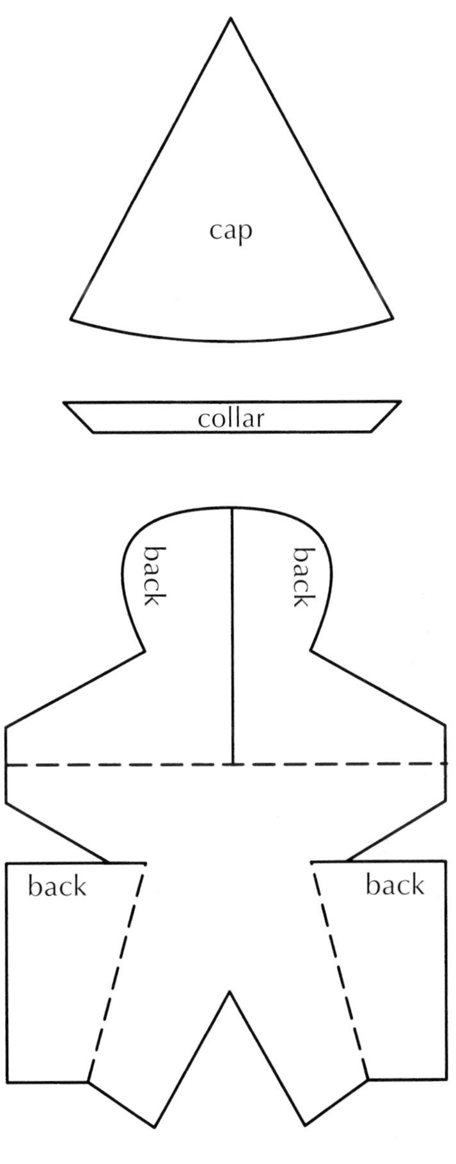


41 *Pattern for Christmas gnome*

## *Jester*

*MATERIALS*

- Pipe-cleaner or wire
- Unvarnished wooden bead with a diameter of 5/8 in (16 mm)
- Unspun wool
- Pieces of felt
- Little bell

*METHOD*

See the *Christmas gnome* for instructions on how to make the pipe-cleaner frame. Wrap some thinly teased unspun wool loosely around the frame.

The dark-red jester in Figure 43 has a suit which consists of a left and a right half of the same colour (see the pattern in Figure 42b). Cut out the pattern of the suit twice using two layers of felt. Open out the felt and lay the frame between the two layers, the front and back. Sew the two halves of the suit together, taking care to use small stitches. The jester's hands and feet are attached to the rest of the suit. Tie up the hands at the wrists and the feet at the ankles.

Cut out the collar in Figure 42a, gather it, lay it around the neck and sew the collar on to the jester's back. Cut out the jester's cap from a double piece of felt, sew it together and glue it on to the head. You can attach a little bell or a coloured bead on to the conical cap.

The dolls illustrated are about 3 in (7–8 cm) high without caps.

Instead of the jester's one-piece suit, you can make a suit, collar and cap out of two halves of different colours. This time, cut out the felt, one piece at a time, and first sew the two halves of the different colours together so that you get a front and a back. Finish off the jester as before.

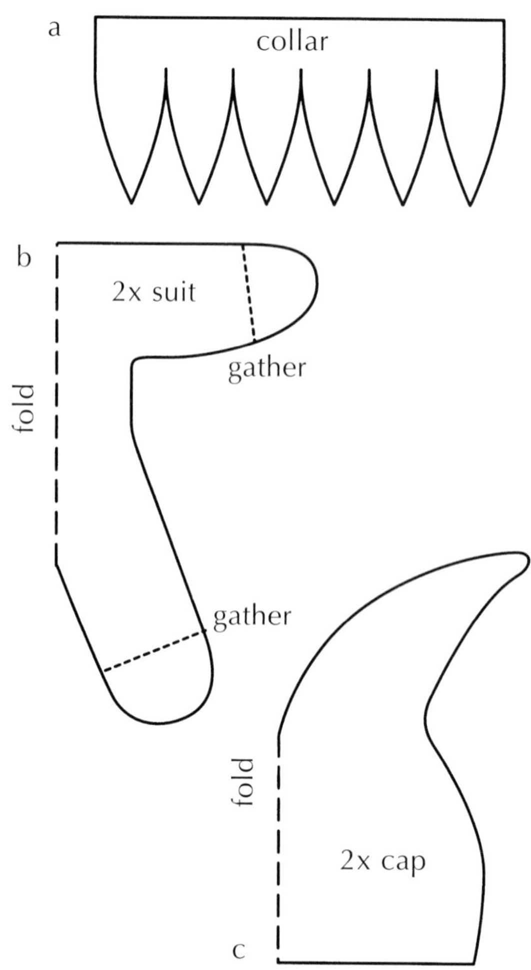


42 *Pattern for jester*

43 *Jesters*

## *Pipe-cleaner man*

*MATERIALS*

- Pipe-cleaners
- Unvarnished wooden bead with a diameter of 1/2 in (12 mm)
- Pink cotton knit
- Pieces of felt
- Little red beads

*METHOD*

Begin in the same way as for the basic model (page 36, Figure 36), but use a longer piece of pipe-cleaner. This is because this time the pipe-cleaner is not cut off but bent round for the arms and legs, so that they are made out of a double pipe-cleaner (Figure 44a). If the pipe-cleaner is too long, wind the excess around the body.

Clothe the hands with a small piece of pink cotton knit and secure this at the wrists.

The pattern in Figure 44 consists of a jacket, two trouser legs and two shoes.

First make the shoes by sewing the two pieces of felt together, pulling them up over the feet and tying them on.

Take the two trouser legs, fold them around the legs and sew them up. They should reach up to the armpits. Sew the tops of the trouser legs together to make a pair of trousers.

Cut out the jacket making sure that the neck-opening is big enough to push the head through. Sew up the front of the jacket and attach the beads.

Sew the hair on the middle of the head only. After cutting the loops you can glue the hair on to the head in locks (Figure 45).

The doll is about 3 1/2 in (9 cm) long.

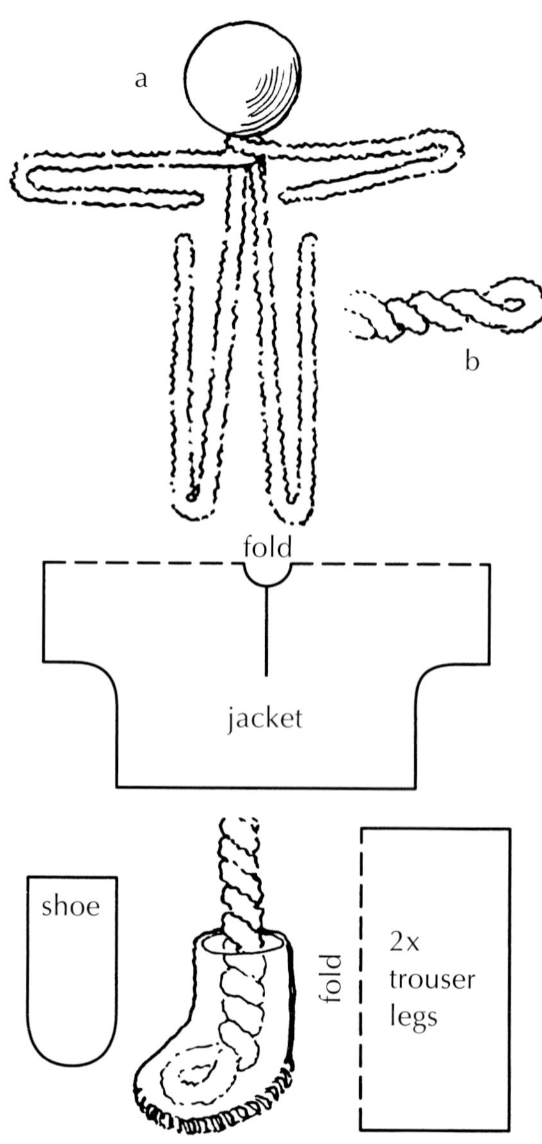


44 *Pattern for pipe-cleaner man*

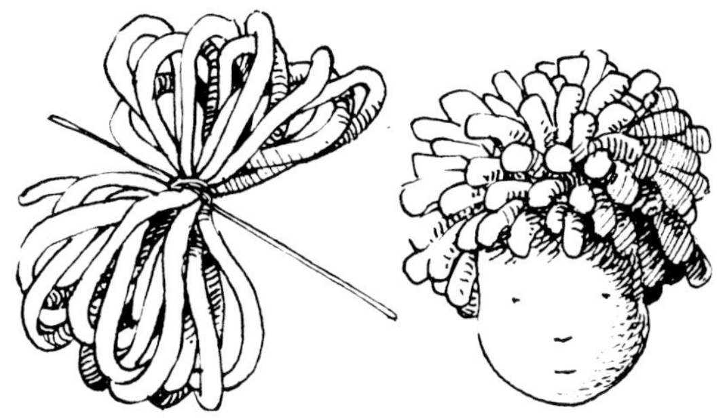

45 *Making the hair*

46 *Pipe-cleaner man*

## *The man in the moon*

*MATERIALS*

- Pipe-cleaners
- Unvarnished bead with 5/8 in (16 mm) diameter
- Pieces of felt
- Unspun wool
- Small red beads with a diameter of 1/8 in (4 mm)
- An iron ring with a diameter of 3 1/2 in (8–9 cm), or a piece of cane

*METHOD*

See Figure 40 for instructions on how to make the basic frame. Thinly teased wool is then wound around the frame, as was the case with the *Christmas gnome*.

Sew the trousers firmly on to the man (see the pattern in Figure 47). Gather the trouser leg in at the foot, draw in the thread and secure it before attaching the beads to the material to make the feet.

Cut open the jacket at the back and sew it firmly on to the doll. Gather in the ends of the sleeves and attach the small beads for hands (Figure 48).

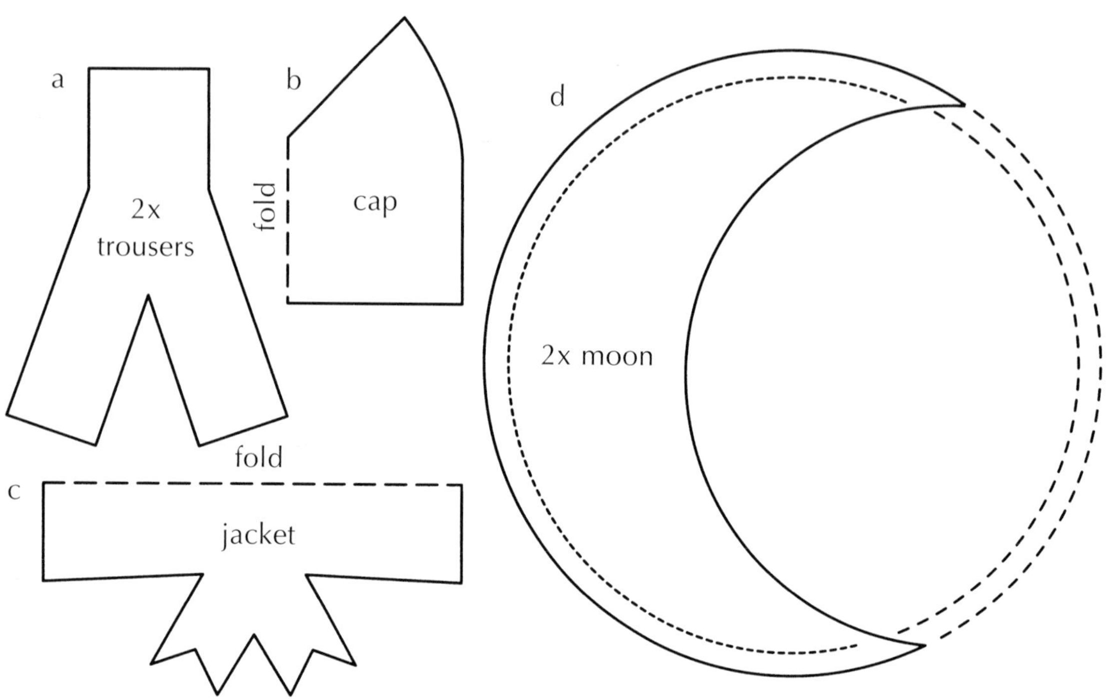


47 *Pattern for man in the moon*

Give the man some unspun wool for hair.

Without his cap the gnome is 2 1/2 in (6 cm) tall.

To make the cap, cut out the material using the pattern, sew it up at the back and glue it on to the head.

Take the iron ring or make a ring from cane and wind yellow wool around it. Lay the ring on a piece of felt so that you can draw a crescent moon, which you then cut out and sew on to the ring. Tie a golden thread to the ring and hang it up.

48 *Man in the moon*

## *Wooden doll with moveable arms and legs*

*MATERIALS*

- A wooden doll (see *Method*)
- Pieces of felt
- Knitting wool for the hair

*METHOD*

In craft shops you can buy dolls with wooden heads, bodies, hands and feet, but whose arms and legs are made of wire wrapped in cord. These dolls can stand with their arms and legs bent in various postures (Figure 50). Dolls made with pipe-cleaners can be shaped into various postures but they are usually unable to stand.

Begin by dressing the feet. Glue a piece of felt on to the sole of the foot and trim around each foot, leaving a margin of about 1/16 in (1–2 mm). Cut out the tops of the shoes following the pattern in Figure 49c and glue these on to the feet too. Trim off the surplus felt and sew the tops to the felt soles.

Cut out the trousers as in the pattern in Figure 49d and sew them on to the back of the doll. If necessary, slant both ends in slightly at the waist. The trousers should reach almost to the armpits.

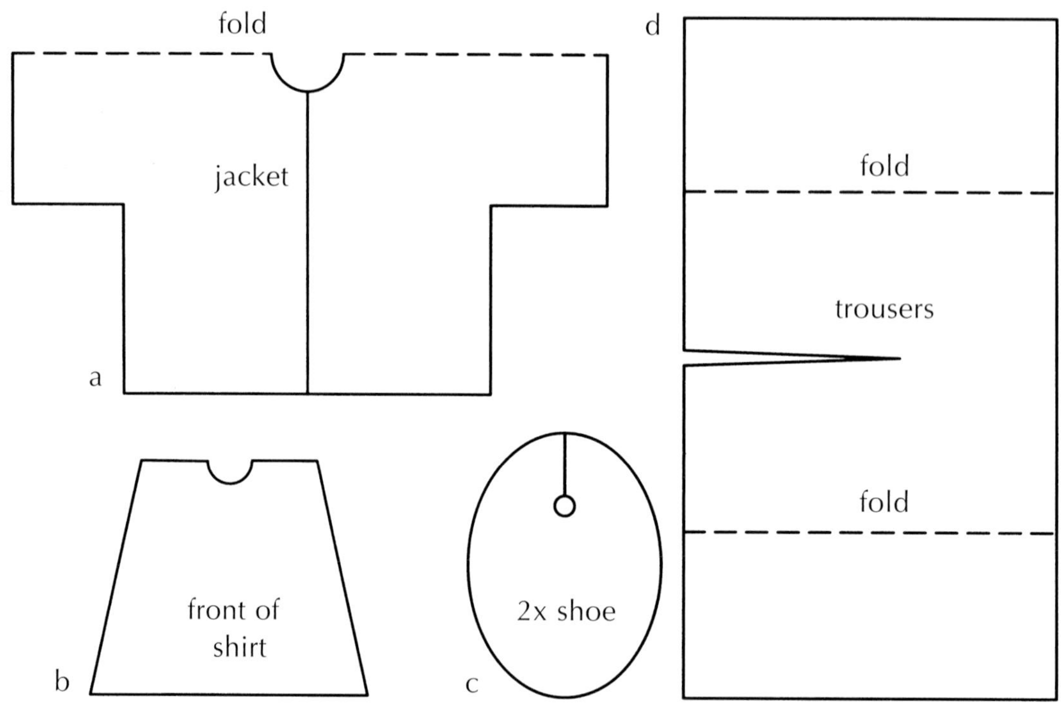


49 *Pattern for wooden doll*

Because the doll has a jacket he only needs the front of a shirt (Figure 49b). Sew the top of the shirt around the neck with a few stitches and sew the bottom on to the trousers.

Finally cut out the jacket as in Figure 49a. Sew up the seams and put it on the doll.

See page 9 for the hair.

50 *Wooden doll*

# Animals and Birds

## Duck

*MATERIALS*

- Felt
- Thin card
- Unspun wool

*METHOD*

The pattern in Figure 52 has two similar sides, two wings, the base, the beak and the eyes.

Follow the pattern to cut out the base parts from pieces of felt.

Use a piece of card for the base so that the bird will stand.

Sew up the head and neck, making sure that the beak is secured between both sides of the head. Before sewing up the rest of the body, fill the head and neck with some unspun wool. Keep stuffing the body as you go on sewing it up. Leave the underside half-open and sew it up only when the body is fully stuffed.

Take the wings and sew them on to the front of the body.

Cut out a small circle for the eye and sew it in place. If you prefer, you can embroider the eyes.

The ducks shown are 2–2 1/4 in (5–6 cm) wide (Figure 51).

## Swan

*MATERIALS*

- Felt
- Thin card
- Unspun wool
- Red embroidery thread

*METHOD*

Unlike the duck, for which the head, neck and body are in one piece with the wings sewn on to the body, the swan consists of three parts: firstly the head, neck and wings, secondly the rest of the body, and thirdly the base. Cut out the base following the pattern in Figure 53 plus a little piece of card to stabilize it.

First sew the head and neck together and fill them with unspun wool.

Then partly sew up the body, leaving an opening large enough to stuff wool into the body.

Once the body is fully stuffed, sew it up. Insert the piece of card at the base and sew it in, as for the duck.

Now bring the wings (with neck and head attached) over the body and secure them to the underside of the body. Sew two small circles of felt on to the head for eyes, or embroider them. Embroider the beak in the same way.

The swan is about 3 1/4 in (8 cm) wide and 3 1/4 in (8 cm) high.

51 *Ducks and swan*

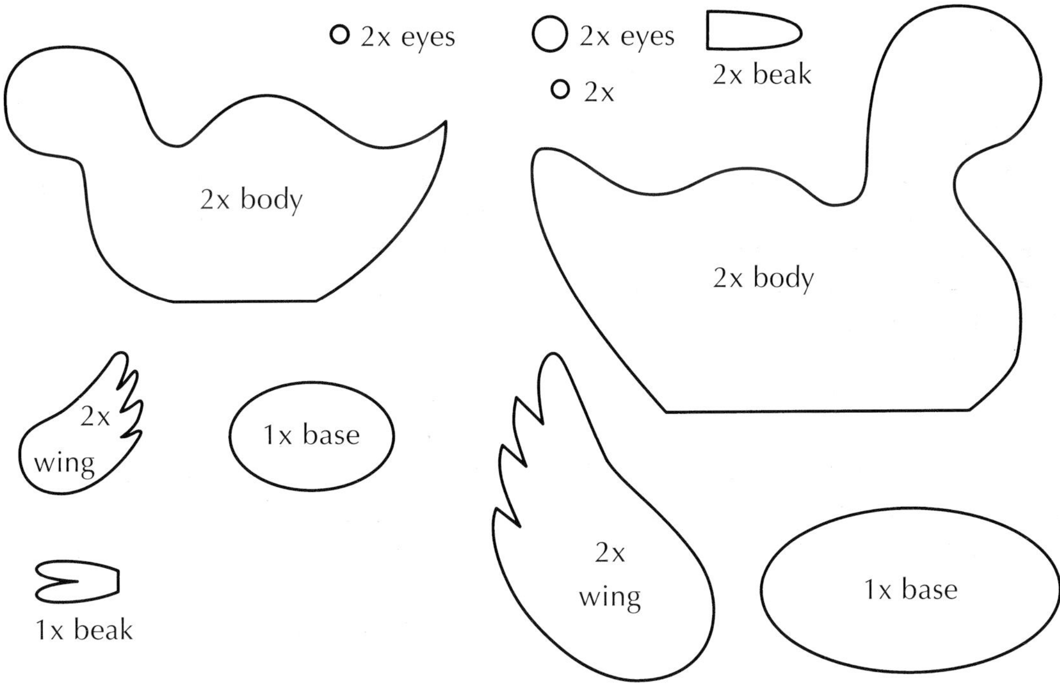


52 *Pattern for ducks*

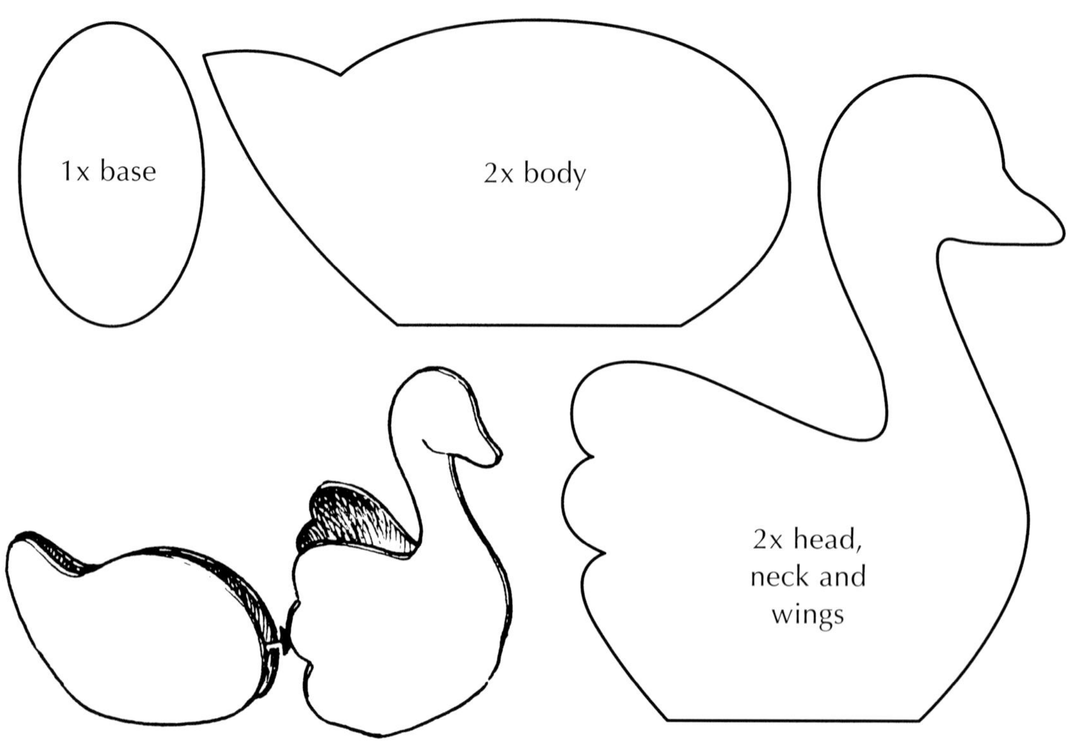


53 *Pattern for swan*

## Seal

*MATERIALS*

- Pieces of felt
- Unspun wool
- Beads

*METHOD*

The pattern in Figure 55 has one piece for the head, the body and the flippers, and one piece for the belly and the flippers. There is also an inset piece for the head.

Cut out the pattern and sew together the two belly pieces, which together make the underside of the body.

First sew the inset piece of the head to one of the sides and then join both side pieces (with the inset piece) together halfway down the back, leaving the rest of the back open.

Now lay the two pieces that make up the belly inside the rest of the body with the edge inwards. Sew the breast, the front flippers, the sides and the hind flippers together in that order. Stuff the seal and then sew up the back.

To finish off, you can use red beads for the eyes, and embroider on some whiskers (Figure 54).

54 *Seal*

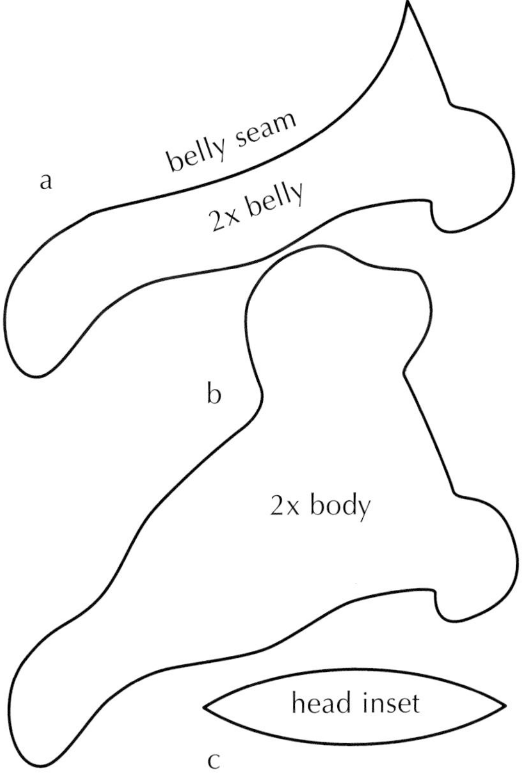


55 *Pattern for seal*

56 *Bird*

## *Bird*

*MATERIALS*

- Piece of felt
- Unspun wool
- Pipe-cleaner

*METHOD*

The pattern in Figure 57 has three pieces: the upper part of the body with the wings, a separate piece for the wings, and two separate side pieces for the head and body.

Sew the detached wings to the underside of the body with wings. The material for the wings is now double so it should be quite firm. Despite this, the wings will soon hang down a little. If you do not want them to do this, either sew in a pipe-cleaner along the front of the wings or insert a thin piece of card between them.

Now take the two sides of the head and body and sew them together at the bottom. The two sides now make the beak, head, body and tail. Sew them on to the top of the body. Leave a little bit at the tail open for stuffing the body with unspun wool. This ensures that the wings are not stuffed.

Sew up the body and embroider the eyes. Use orange or red embroidery thread for the beak. Embroider the end of the beak first so that you can then wind the thread around the beak and tie it off.

Pass a thread right through the body so that the bird can fly (hang). Before tying it off, make sure that it hangs effectively.

Birds are suitable for using in mobiles. This can consist of a hoop on which a number of birds are hung, but it can also be a more intricate mobile consisting of a number of separate rods.

You can add variety by changing the size and colour of the birds.

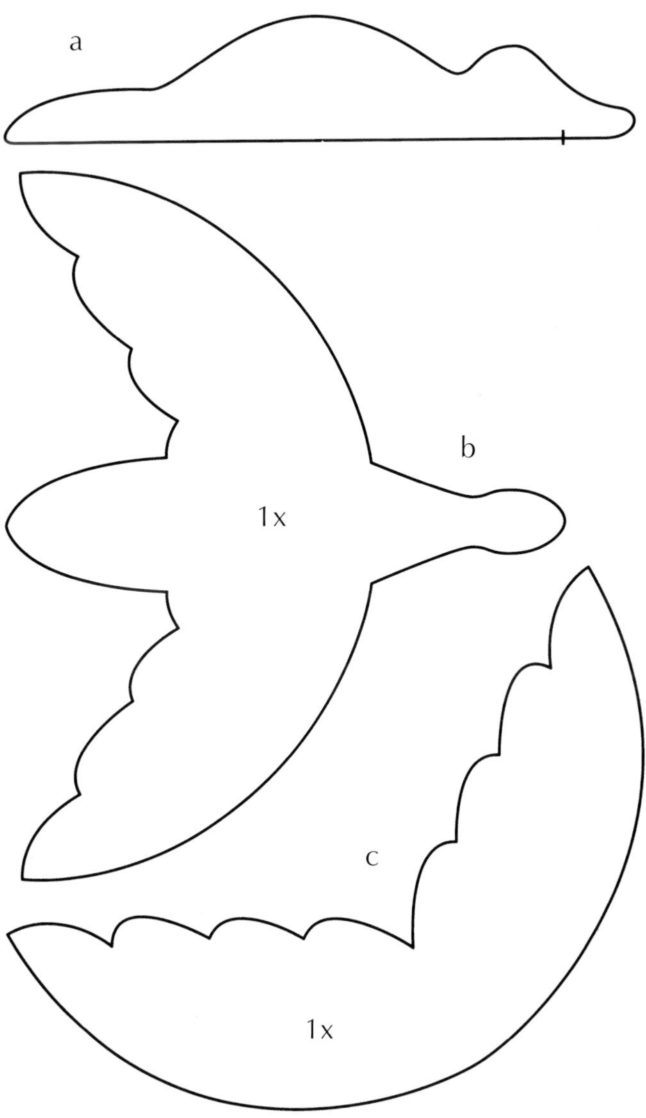


57 *Pattern for bird*

58 *Mobile with butterflies*

## *Mobile with butterflies*

*MATERIALS*

- Pieces of felt
- Pipe-cleaners
- Thin green wire
- Small beads

*METHOD*

The butterflies have wings made of two layers of felt glued together and sewn around the edge if necessary.

Figure 58 shows how you can use your imagination to vary the shape of the wings and also the shapes cut into the wings. It is fun to choose attractive colour combinations for the different layers of felt, which are revealed by the shapes cut into the wings.

The inside of the body consists of a piece of pipe-cleaner about 2 in (5 cm) long. Make two antennae about 3/4 in (2 cm) long from a piece of thin (green) wire. Thread a bead on to each end of this and wind the ends of the wire back around the beads. Bend the ends of the pipe-cleaner and attach the middle to make two antennae.

Now clothe the pipe-cleaner with a narrow strip of brown felt about 2 1/4 x 1/2 in (6 x 1.5 cm). Then wind coloured thread or woollen yarn around the body. The gap between the threads should be about 1/4 in (5 mm). Sew the wings on to the body.

Hanging up the butterflies — as for example on a round hoop wrapped in wool — requires some care. The butterflies in Figure 58 are hung by making a square out of thin wire. Two opposite sides of the square are then sewn on to the butterfly, one side on to each wing. Two threads can then attach the square of wire to the hoop above. The square of wire can be bent to allow the butterfly to hang well, the wire keeping the wings open (Figure 60).

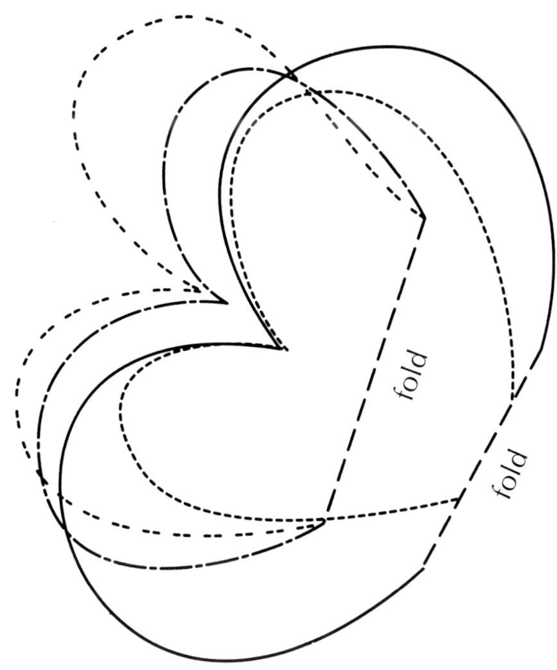


59 *Pattern for butterfly wings*

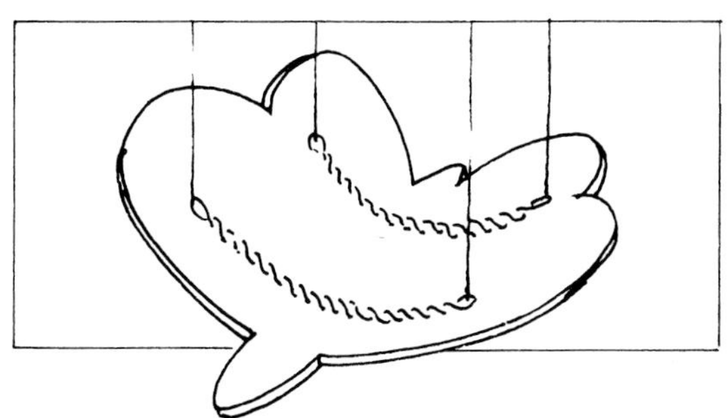

60 *Hanging the butterfly*

61 *Snails*

## *Snail*

*MATERIALS*

- Piece of felt
- Unspun wool
- Long pipe-cleaner or thin wire
- Thin card

*METHOD*

The pattern in Figure 63 consists of the snail's body, shell and two antennae. The body consists of a base and the two sides, all as one piece.

It is essential to stick a piece of card at the base of the body, otherwise the snail will fall over with its top-heavy shell. Sew up the snail, leaving a small opening for stuffing in the unspun wool.

Take a long strip of felt, tapered along one side, for the shell (Figure 62). You will also need a pipe-cleaner about 8 in (20 cm) long or two pipe-cleaners joined together. Alternatively, you can use a piece of wire with the ends bent round.

The coil of the shell has to be thicker at the bottom than at the top. You must therefore wind the unspun wool around the pipe-cleaner more thickly at what is to be the bottom end, thinning it out gradually towards the other end. Make sure the felt fits around tightly and sew it on securely.

Now wind the whole tube around to make the shell (Figure 63). Sew the coils together and sew the shell on to the body.

Cut out two small pieces of felt for the antennae, curl them up firmly, secure them with a few stitches and then sew them on to the head.

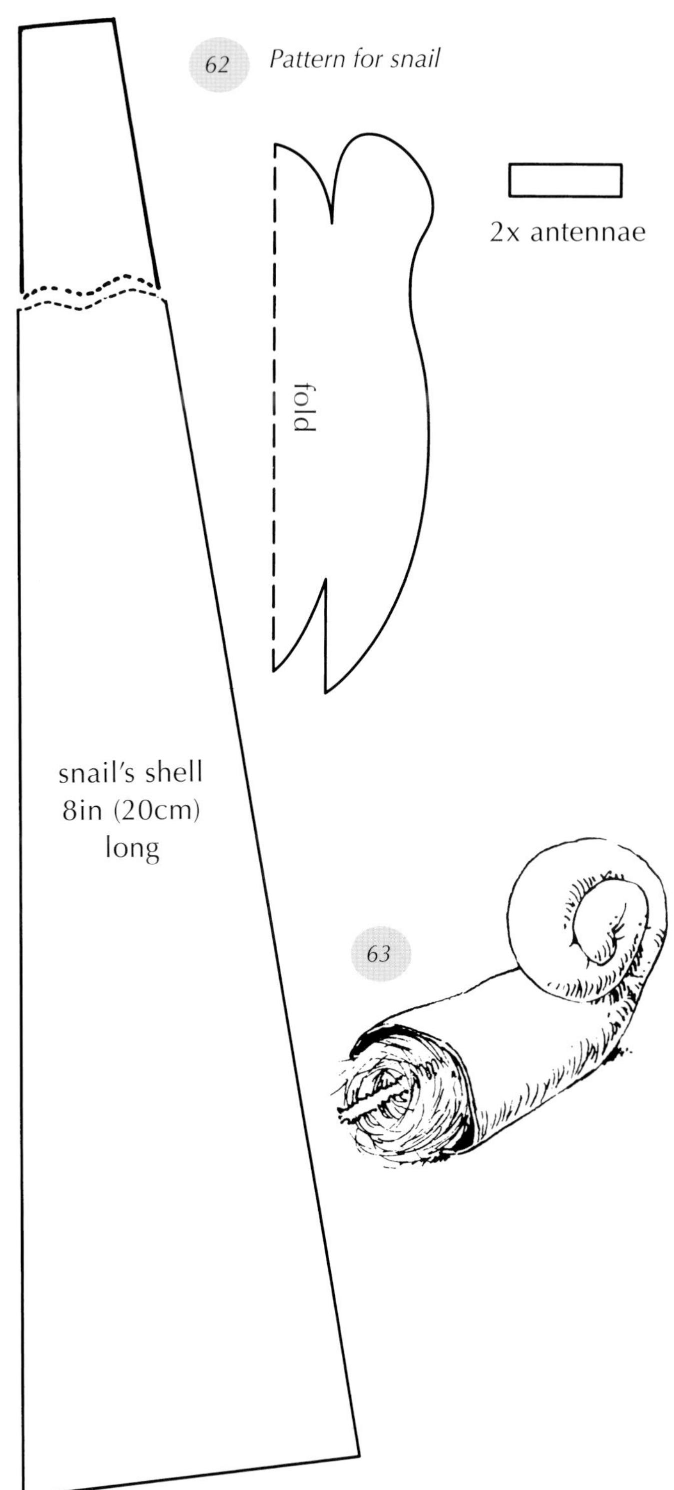


62 *Pattern for snail*

63

64 *Sitting cat*

65 *Mouse*

## *Sitting cat*

*MATERIALS*

- Pieces of felt
- Unspun wool
- Pipe-cleaner
- A small bell
- Thin card

*METHOD*

Cut out the eight parts of the pattern in Figure 66a–f. Take the inset piece for the head and back, and sew the head part between the two side pieces. Stuff the head with teased wool.

Now go on sewing the body on to the back part, and sew the inset for the paws between the two side pieces. Stuff the body with teased wool. Cut out a piece of thin card 1/16 in (2 mm) smaller than the felt base and glue this on to the base. Sew the base on to the body.

Now comes the tail. Sew up one of the short sides and the two long sides of the tail and insert a pipe-cleaner before sewing up the last short side. Sew the tail on to the body and the ears on to the head. Embroider the eyes and whiskers. If you wish, add a ribbon and a bell.

## *Mouse*

*MATERIALS*

- A piece of felt
- Unspun wool
- Thin card

*METHOD*

The pattern for the mouse in Figure 66h–j consists of five parts: the body, two sides and two ears. Cut out the pieces and glue a piece of card on to the inside of the body part. The card should be 1/16 in (2 mm) smaller than the body part.

Sew the sections together, leaving the hind part slightly open for stuffing. Sew up the opening once the body has been stuffed.

Finish off by sewing on the ears and embroidering the nose and whiskers. Crochet a tail and sew it on.

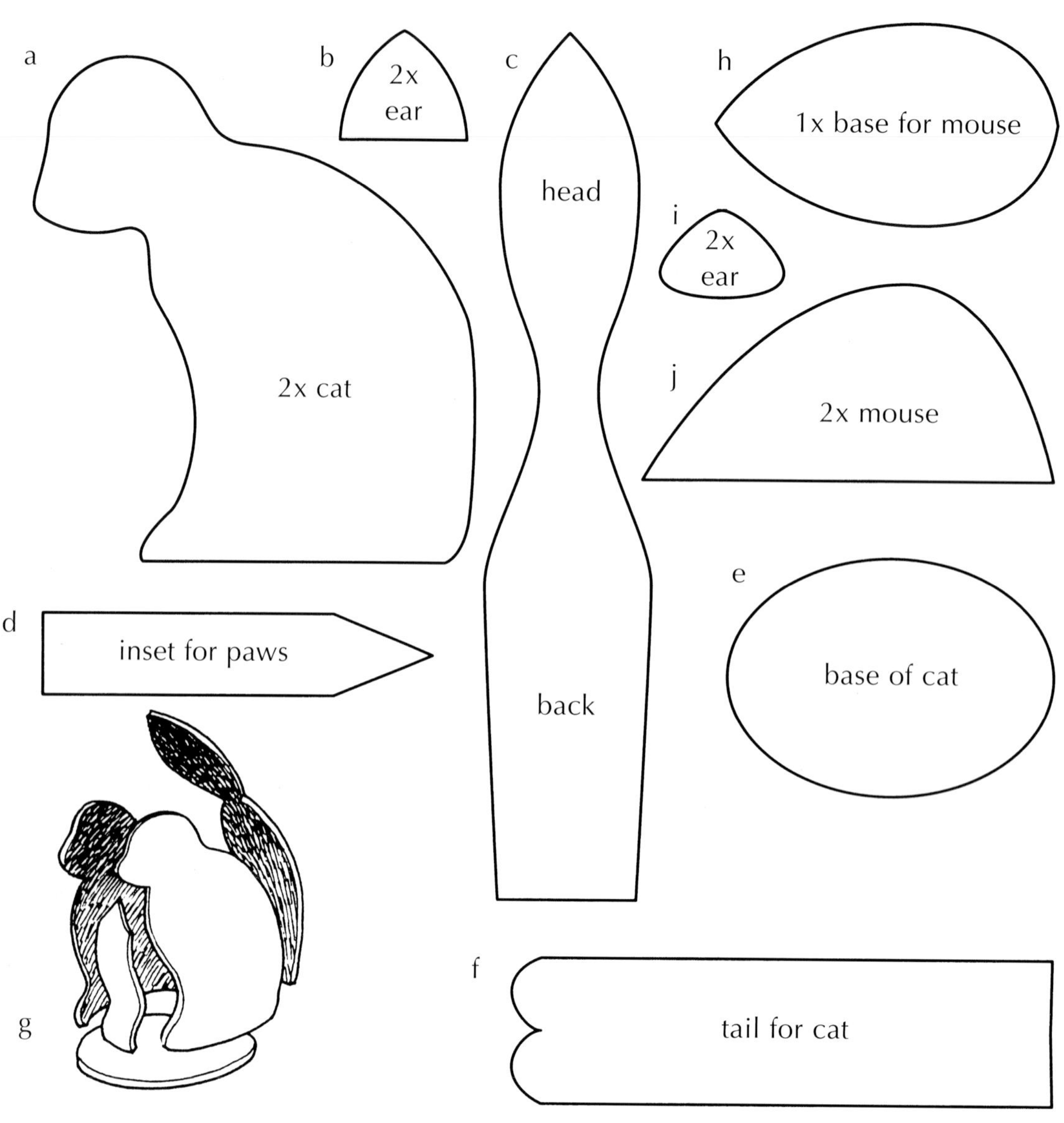


66 *Pattern for cat and mouse*

## *Dog*

*MATERIALS*

- Piece of felt
- Unspun wool

*METHOD*

Cut out the pattern in Figure 67. It consists of two side pieces, a belly piece, an inset piece for the head and two ears.

First sew up the seams of the tail and stuff it with wool, leaving the rest of the body wide open. Then sew up the back seam of the body, legs, underside and front. Stuff the legs. Secure the inset piece for the head and stuff the head. Stuff the body and sew up the back.

Cut out the floppy ears and sew them on to the head. The ears can be the same colour as the body or a different colour.

Finish off the dog by embroidering the eyes and nose. If you wish you can give him a collar (Figure 68).

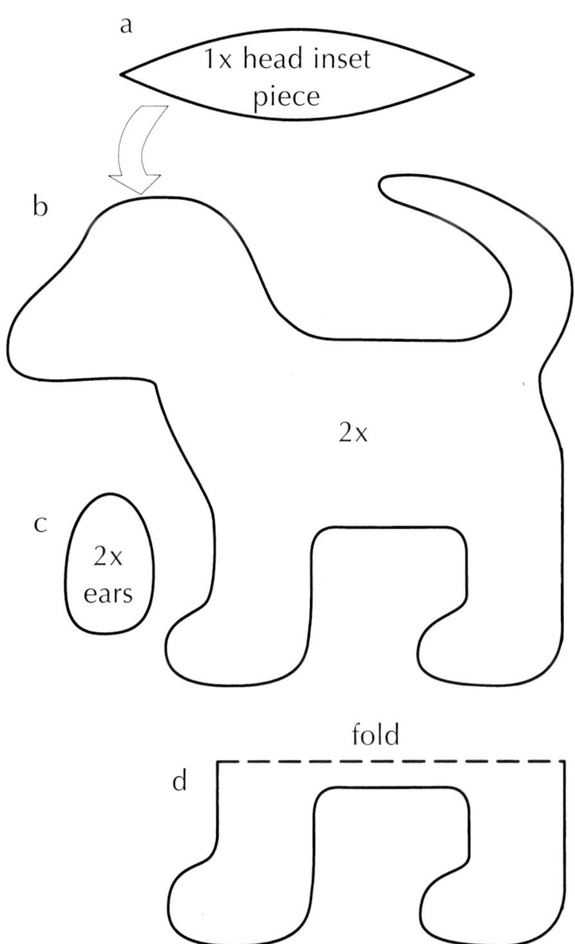


67 *Pattern for dog*

68 *Two dogs*

## *Another dog*

*MATERIALS*

- Pieces of felt
- Unspun wool

*METHOD*

The pattern in Figure 69f–i consists of two side pieces, an inset piece for the head, ears and tail. Cut the pieces out and fold in the insides of the paws. Now trim the soles of the paws, sew them up and fill the legs.

Sew the two parts and the head inset together, leaving the underside of the body still open for stuffing. Sew up the body after you have stuffed it.

Sew the tail and the two ears on to the dog, and embroider the eyes and the nose.

## *Horse*

*MATERIALS*

- Piece of felt
- Unspun wool
- Knitting wool

*METHOD*

The pattern for the horse (Figure 69a–e) consists of two sides, a belly piece, the ears and the base of the hooves. In addition the horse has a blanket, a saddle and a girth.

Cut out the parts. Lay the belly piece between the two side pieces and sew them together. Sew a hoof base on to each leg and stuff the legs. After that you can sew up the rest of the horse's body, leaving a little opening in the back for stuffing. After you have stuffed the body, sew it up.

Now sew on the ears. Embroider the harness and the eyes with some wool and make the mane and tail out of thin wool. Finally, attach a blanket (2 3/4 x 1 1/2 in/7 x 3.5 cm) and a saddle and girth (2 1/2 x 3/8 in/ 6.5 x 1 cm) to the horse's back.

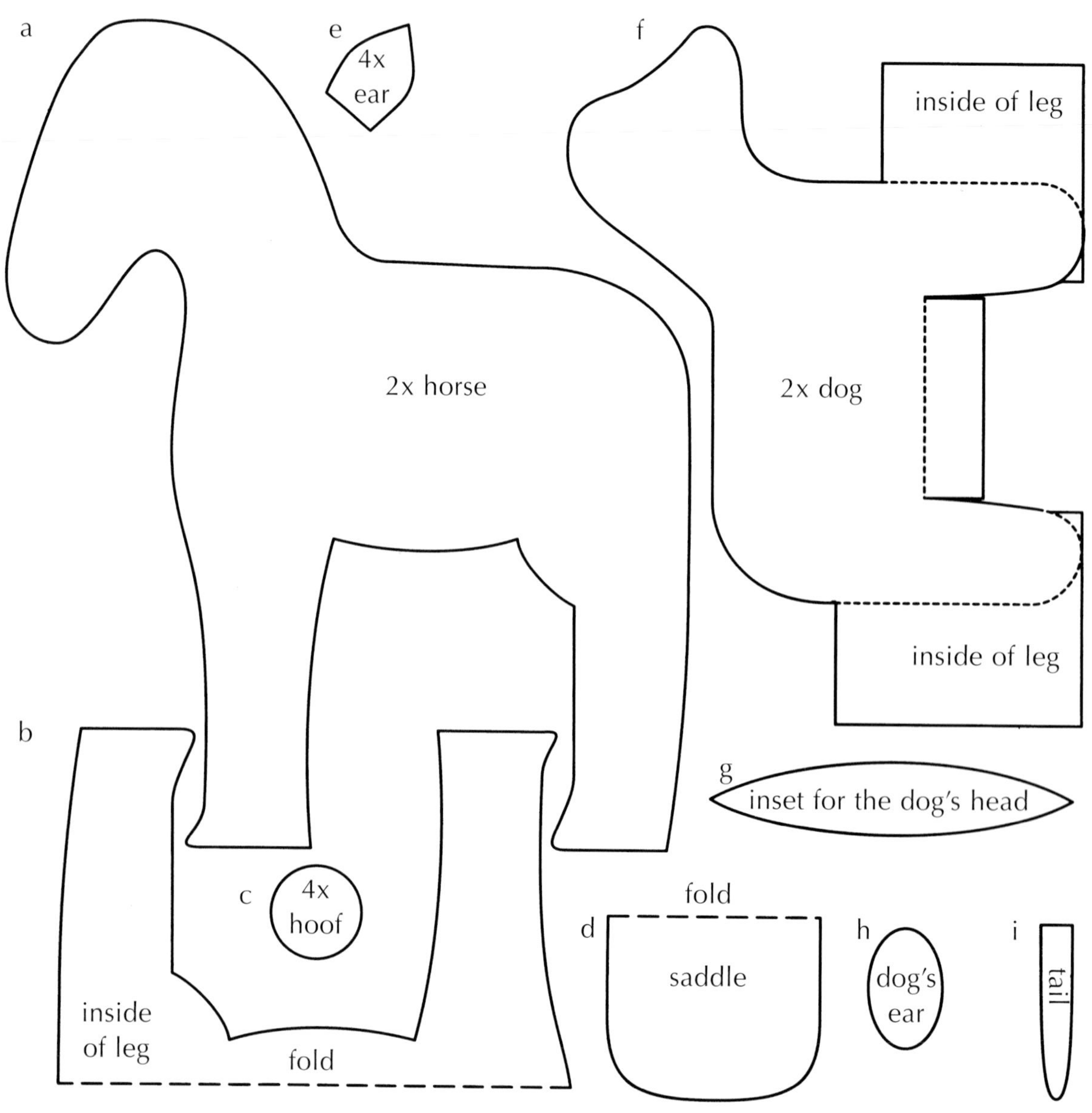


69 *Pattern for another dog and a horse*

70 *Horse*

## *Cockerel*

*MATERIALS*

- Pieces of felt
- Unspun wool
- Thin card
- Beads

*METHOD*

The cockerel's body consists of four parts: two sides, an inset piece for the top and a base. The other items in Figure 73 are adornments, such as the tail-feathers and comb.

Cut out the parts of the pattern. First sew the tail-feathers (Figure 73d) on to the two sides of the cockerel. Then sew the extra feathers (Figure 73f) on to the wings (Figure 73e), and finally sew the two wings on to the side pieces.

Sew the brown lower parts of the eyes on to the head (Figure 72).

To make the body, take the two sides and sew the inset piece between them as shown in Figure 71.

Stuff the cockerel with teased unspun wool and then sew up the front. Finally, give him a comb of double felt and two gills (Figure 73g). The eyes are made from beads.

In Figure 72 the cockerel has a disc of wood to stand on. The felt base (Figure 73b) is glued on to this.

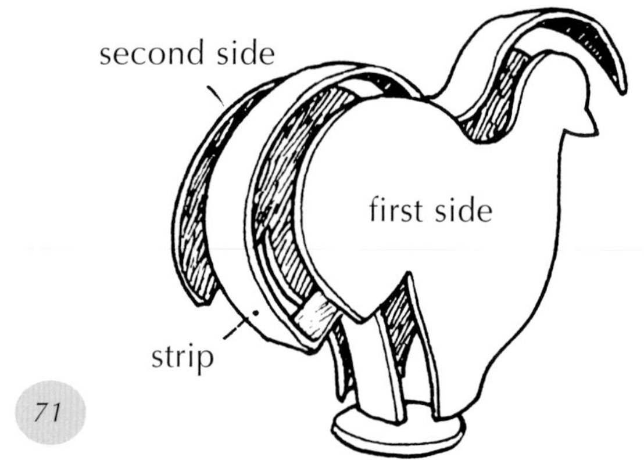


71

72 *Cockerel*

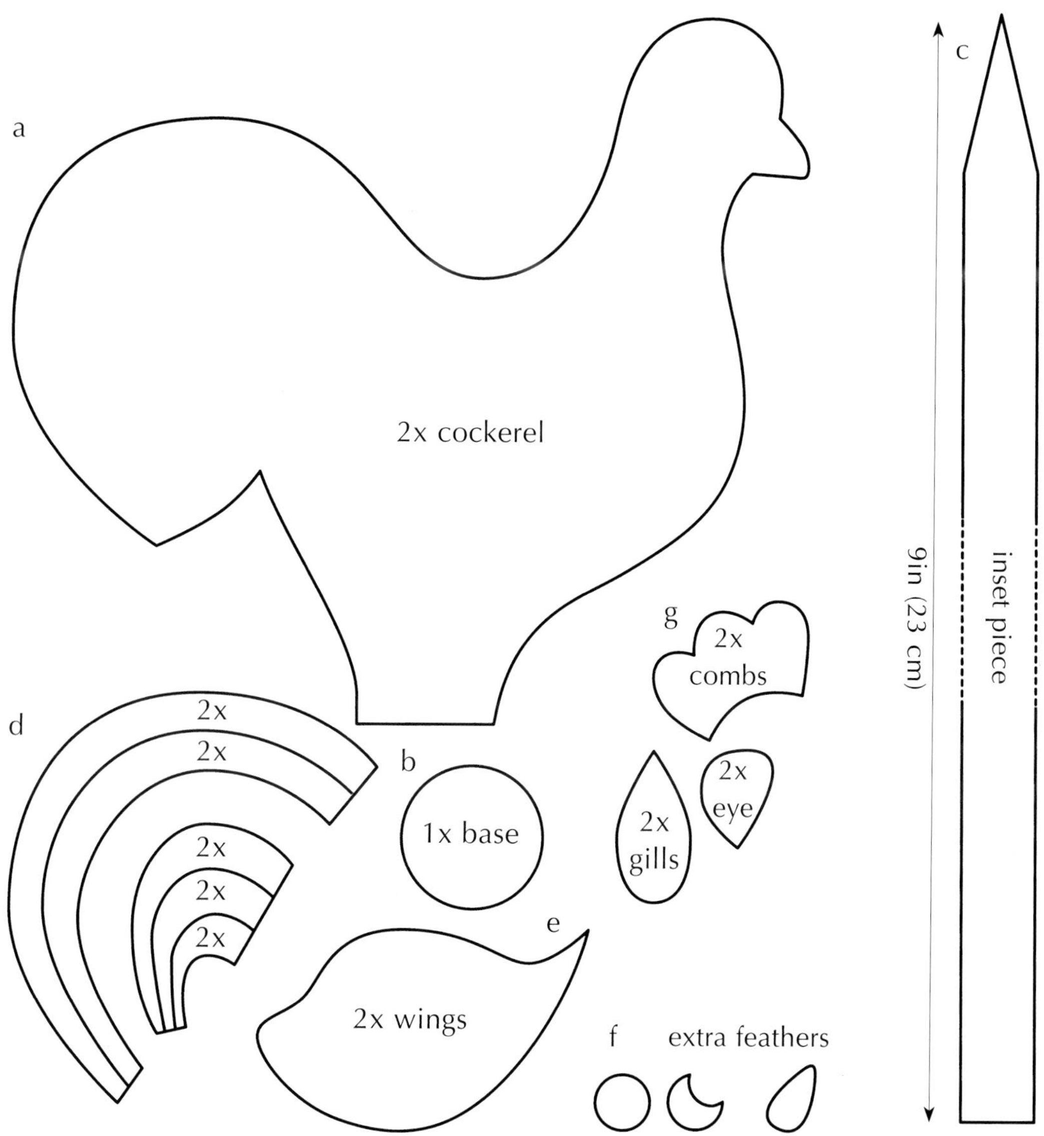


73 *Pattern for cockerel*

74 *Underwater tapestry scene*

# Tapestries

## Simple tapestry

*MATERIALS*

- Pieces of felt
- Larger pieces of fabric

*METHOD*

The choice of background for the tapestry will partly depend on the shape and size you have chosen. Pure woollen felt is rather expensive, so for a larger tapestry it is feasible to make the backcloth from another material. For smaller tapestries, felt is more suitable.

Because felt can be cut and does not fray, even very young children can make their own tapestries by sewing the cut-out shapes on to the backcloth.

You can make the tapestry as complicated as you wish. The fish tapestry shown in Figure 74 is made with fish shapes sewn on to the backcloth and then more detail embroidered on top. The tapestry is 18 1/2 x 17 3/4 in (47 x 45 cm). Although fish patterns are given in Figures 75 and 76, you can of course devise your own designs.

75 *Fish patterns*

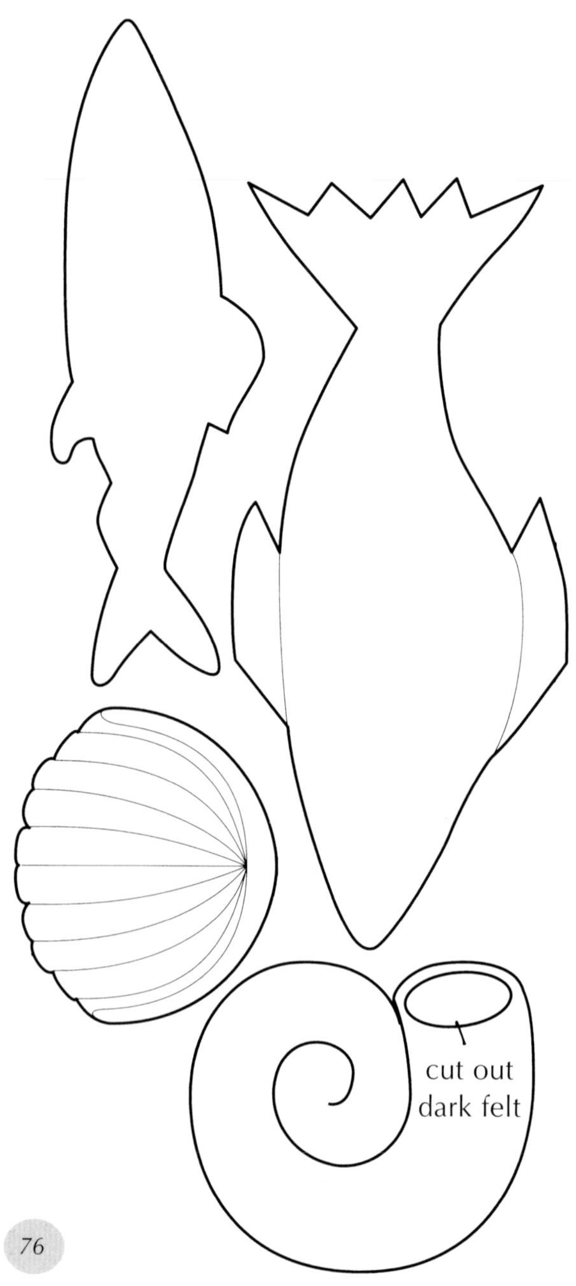


76

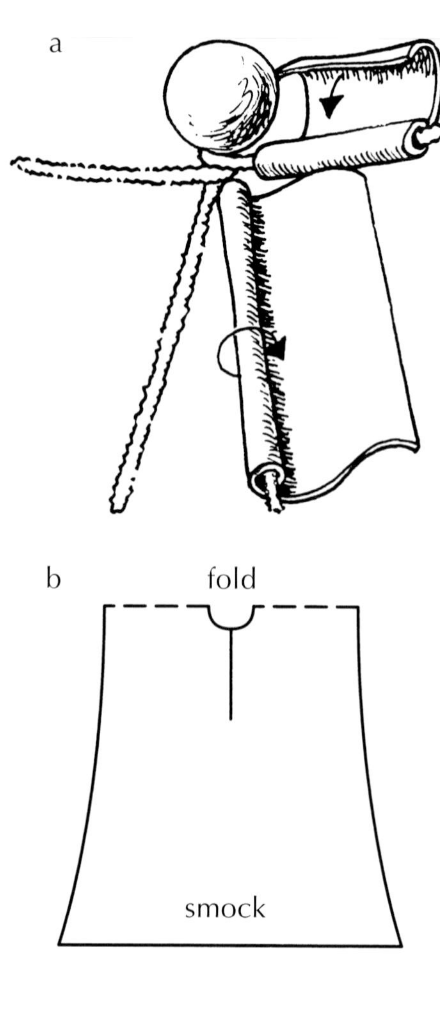


77 *Pattern for the gnome*

## *A gnome in a landscape*

*MATERIALS*

- Pieces of felt
- Strips of wood for the frame
- A piece of card
- Pipe-cleaners
- Unspun wool
- Unvarnished wooden beads with a diameter of 3/4 x 1/2 in (20 and 12 mm)

*METHOD*

The dimensions for this tapestry are about 8 x 7 in (20 x 18 cm). The gnome (including his conical hat) is about 5 1/2 in (14 cm) tall.

The tapestry in Figure 78 uses a wooden frame about 1 1/2 in deep and 1/4 in wide (4 x 5mm) instead of just having a backcloth on to which everything is sewn. All sorts of things, such as a landscape, water, a house or the inside of a room, can be sewn or embroidered on to the backcloth. The advantage of having a wooden frame is that you can add three-dimensional figures in front of a background, such as a gnome, a cat, a snail and so on.

The tapestry shown is very simple, with pieces of felt sewn on to each other. The embroidery is confined to the tree, but it can also be used for flowers and so on.

For the illustration in this book the tapestry has been kept fairly small, but it can of course be made much larger.

When the tapestry is finished it should be stapled immediately on to a wooden frame. If necessary you can glue it on to a piece of card first. If you make the tapestry larger you will have to use thicker strips of wood.

### *The gnome*

The gnome is 4 in (10 cm) tall without his conical hat. His frame is made in the same way as the pipe-cleaner doll in Figure 36, but this time the arms and legs are enclosed in a piece of felt (Figure 78). The pieces of felt are the same length as the arms and legs (up to the armpits) and about 3 1/4 in (8 cm) wide. Wrap the pieces of felt around, with the ends at the back of the doll. Secure these ends on to the back.

Sew the sleeves and trouser legs together so that they sit firmly and make a sort of body. Any resulting unevenness will be covered up when the gnome is dressed.

Cut out the smock in Figure 77 and pull it over the neck. Gather the felt in at the waist and finish off by giving the gnome a belt secured at the back.

Give the gnome a beard and hair from unspun wool and glue them on to the head and face. Cut out the hat, sew it up at the back and glue it to the head.

78 *Gnome in a landscape*

## *A first book*

*MATERIALS*

- Pieces of felt
- Cotton material

*METHOD*

It is a very good idea if a young child's first book is made of cloth rather than paper or cardboard. This means it is nice and soft and cannot hurt the child.

Because small children are inclined to put everything into their mouth, it is important that all the pieces are well sewn on.

First determine the size of the book and the number of pages. A book for a very small child does not need to have many pages. In fact eight or ten pages — which makes four or five opened-out spreads — is plenty. Young children enjoy looking at the same picture over and over again. Keep the pictures as simple and recognizable as possible.

Because pure woollen felt is fairly expensive, the little book in Figure 79 is made from cotton fabric. The pictures can still be made of felt.

Cut out a strip of the material to the intended height of the book and fold the material like a concertina to make the pages.

Unfold the material again and mark the outline of the pages with a pencil or tacking thread.

Now cut out the felt figures and sew them into position on the pages and finish them off with embroidery if necessary.

Fold the strip back into pages again and sew them together. All the pages should now be sewn together at the spine and attached to the cover.

Because only very simple pictures are required for this book, no patterns have been included.

79 *A first book*

## *French knitting*

Children from about six years onwards love to do French knitting (also called frame knitting) and finger crochet with woollen yarn. These are excellent hobbies, which each child can do at their own pace.

*MATERIALS*

- Knitting wool
- Wooden knitting Nancy or bobbin
- Thick darning needle

*METHOD*

Let the end of the yarn hang through the hole in the centre of the knitting Nancy or bobbin and twist it loosely around the first peg or staple (Figure 80a). Now go across the middle of the knitting Nancy to the peg on the left-hand side (Figure 80b) and twist the yarn loosely around it. Do the same with the next peg and the final one on the right-hand side (Figure 80c). Now bring the yarn back to the first peg (Figure 80d).

Now take the loop over the yarn and the peg using the needle (Figure 80e).

From now on always twist the yarn clockwise around the pegs so that the last loop can be taken around the yarn and the peg. In this way you make a cord in the hole of the knitting Nancy. In order to achieve an even cord, it is important to give the yarn hanging from the knitting Nancy a gentle pull from time to time.

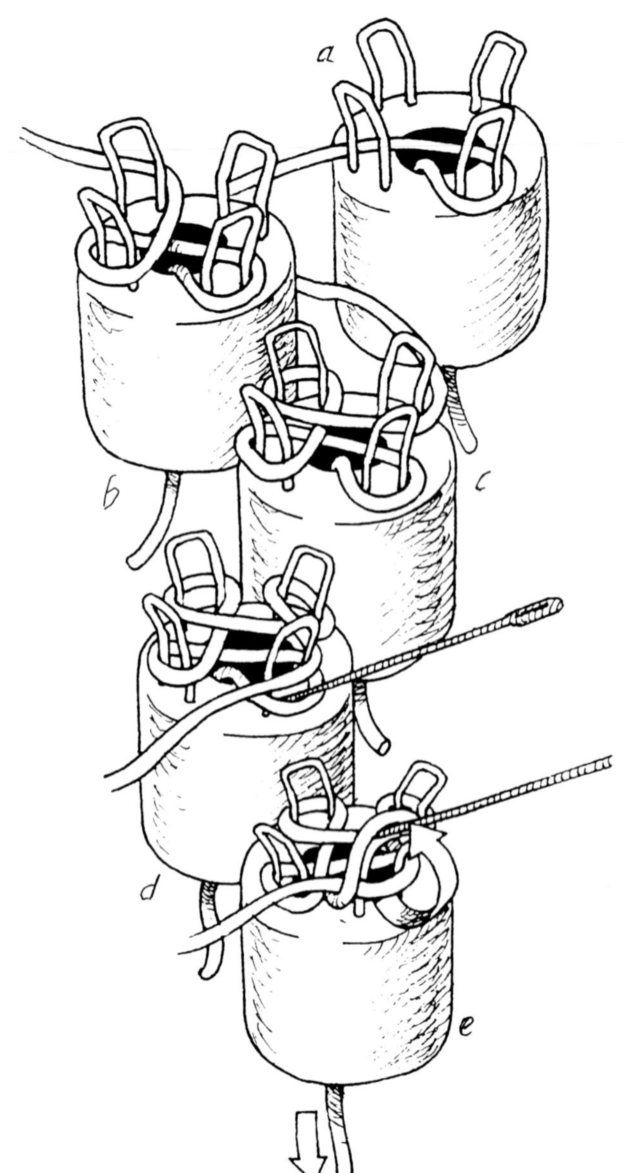


80 *French knitting*

## *Finger crochet*

*MATERIALS*

- Thick knitting wool

*METHOD*

Make a loop with the knitting wool as shown in Figure 81a and hold the two strands with one hand where they cross.

With your other hand pull the yarn through the loop (Figure 81b) and pull gently. Turn the loop over so that the yarn from the ball now sits behind the loop. Pull this through the loop again and now pull the loop tight (Figure 81c).

Continue in this way until you have produced the pattern in Figures 81d and e.

Once the crocheted chain is long enough, cut off the yarn, pull the end through the loop and tighten.

You can make many things with this crocheted chain. Or it can be used for decoration, as in Figure 82 where the sun is made by winding the chain round and round like the shell of a snail. The decoration on the little bag of Figure 83 is also finger crochet.

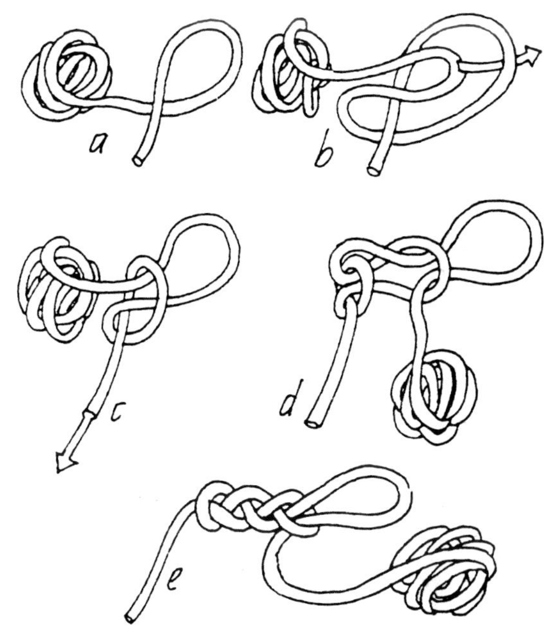


81 *Finger crochet*

## *Tapestry with French knitting*

*MATERIALS*

- Pieces of felt
- Knitting wool
- Wooden knitting Nancy or bobbin
- A thick needle

*METHOD*

This tapestry is also suitable for children to make, but you may need to help them a bit with the sewing up.

Cut out the backcloth of the tapestry and the designs for it. Let the child make an edging with French knitting, allowing them to choose the colours. The house in Figure 82 is also made from a French-knitted cord, while the circle for the sun is finger-crocheted.

82 *Tapestry 12 in x 6 in (30 x 15 cm)*

## *Bag with French-knitted strap*

*MATERIALS*

- Piece of felt
- Thick knitting wool
- Wooden knitting Nancy or bobbin
- Thick needle

83 *Bag with French-knitted strap*

*METHOD*

Take a piece of felt 7 x 4 in (18 x 10 cm) and fold it in two.

Make a design from a finger-crocheted chain and sew it on to one half of the piece of felt for decoration.

Then sew up the two sides and attach the French-knitted cord on to each side.

## *Fir trees and grasses*

*MATERIALS*

- Pieces of felt
- A little strip of wood
- A slice of wood from a log or stick

*METHOD*

The trees described here can make a very attractive background for the dolls and animals explained earlier.

Saw a little strip of wood which is at least 1/2 in (15mm) shorter than the felt tree on to which it will be glued. Fix the strip of wood on to a thin base of wood to make a stand for the tree. The size of the base depends on the size of the tree.

The effect of grass can be created by making cuts into one side of a narrow strip of felt and then gluing this to a piece of wood so that it stands up (Figure 51).

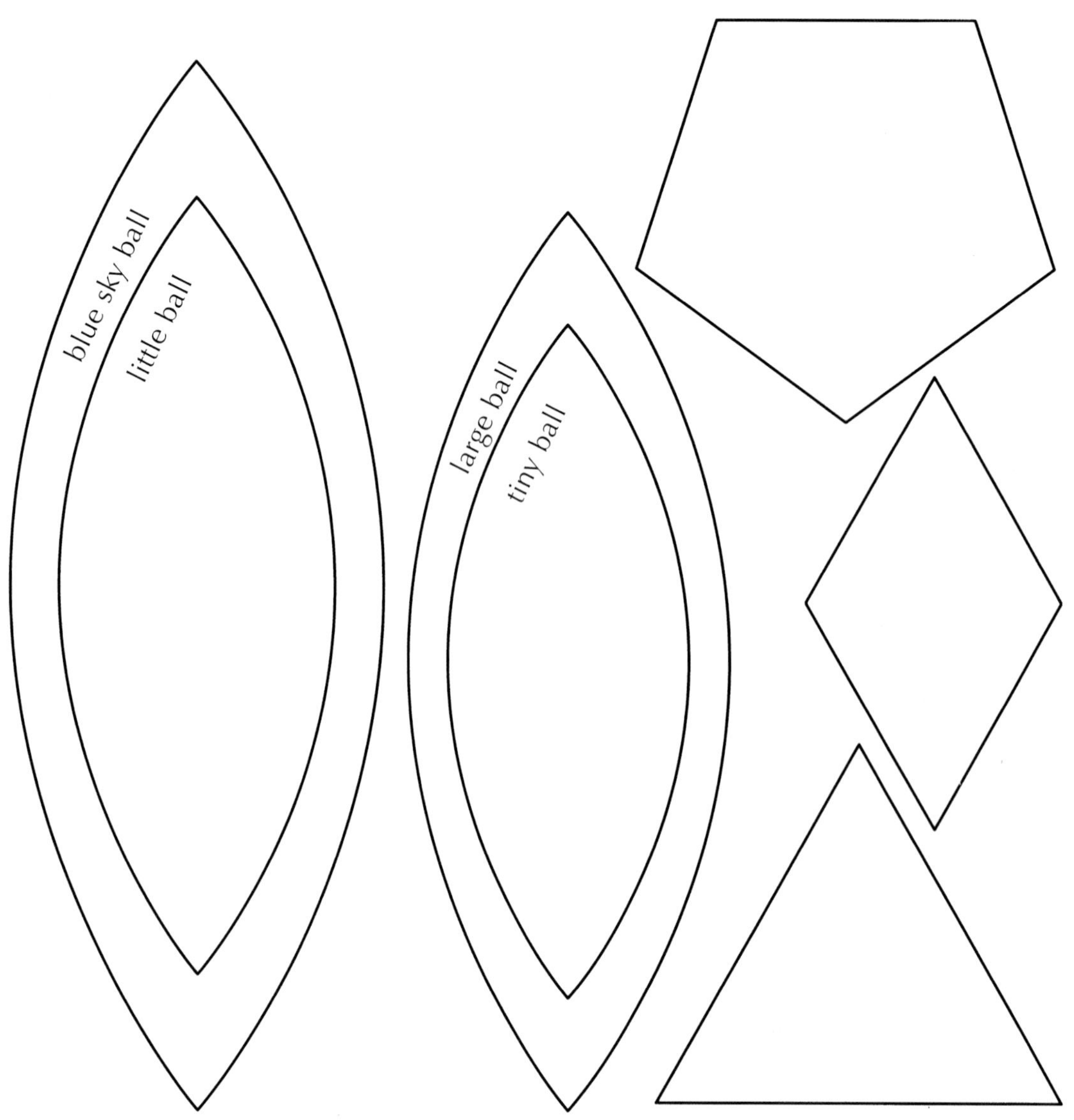


*84 Pattern for felted balls*

# Balls

The balls shown in Figure 85 are made in various ways. The simplest one consists of six sections. But there are also balls made up of twelve pentagons, another of twenty triangles, and another of ten diamonds.

*MATERIALS*

- Pieces of felt
- Unspun wool
- Embroidery thread

*METHOD*

Figure 84 shows the patterns for the various balls. Cut out the required number of parts (see above) and sew them together with small stitches.

Figure 85 shows how different kinds of stitches can be used for sewing up the balls. If you wish, you can use embroidery thread in the same colour as the felt so that the stitches hardly show. Or you can deliberately use a contrasting colour so that the result adds decoration. Page 8 shows various suitable stitches.

Felt can pull apart, so it is advisable to tack the separate pieces of felt together first before sewing the whole ball together.

Leave a piece of felt open before sewing up the ball completely, so that you can stuff the ball with teased unspun wool. Finally sew up the last piece.

You can achieve endless variations by using different colours. You can also make a plain ball and embellish it with embroidery or by sewing on a felt design. This is how the blue sky ball was made, on one side of which is the sun, and on the other the moon and stars.

85 *Felted balls*

86 *Necklaces from left: round disc, (earrings); scrap felt; rolled felt; pennant.*

# Jewellery

## Necklaces and earrings

*MATERIALS*

- Small pieces of felt
- Wire
- Necklace clasps
- Various die-cuts or punches
- Earring hooks or clamps
- Beads

*METHOD*

Making a necklace is an excellent pastime for a rainy afternoon and children can make them themselves. You can use small scraps of felt.

### *Pennant necklace*

The pattern in Figure 87 shows little pennants of various kinds, which are used as the basis for beads. By varying the sizes and shapes of these you can make the necklaces more imaginative.

Cut out the required number of pennants. Roll them around a skewer and sew up the point. Pull out the skewer and thread the bead you have formed on to a wire of the required length. Continue in the same way. Once the necklace is long enough, attach a clasp and hook to each end.

### *Rolled felt and bead necklace*

Rolling up square or rectangular pieces of felt makes quite a different effect from that of the rolled round pennants (Figure 86). Otherwise the method is the same.

Unlike the former necklace, you now thread real beads between the felt beads.

### *Scrap felt and bead necklace*

For this necklace you only need scraps. Cut out little squares of various sizes from the scraps. Thread one square scrap and one bead alternately on to the wire until you have the required length of necklace (Figure 86). You can use any shape you wish for this necklace, and you do not have to be restricted to squares.

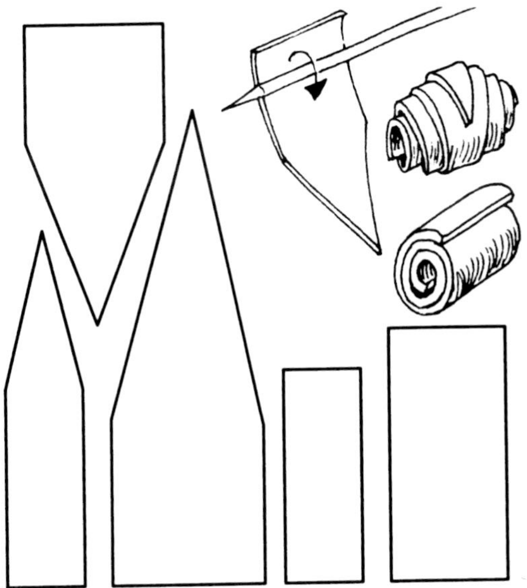

87 *Pattern for jewellery*

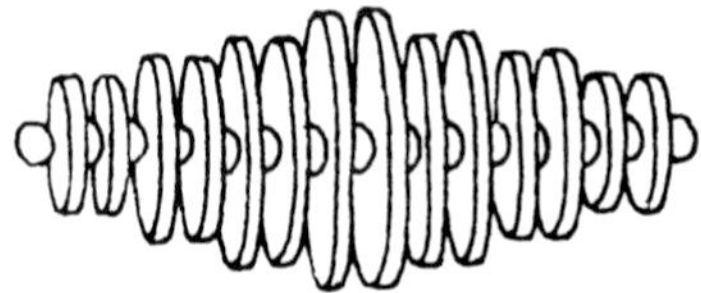

88 *Detail of round disc necklace and earrings*

Advancing from the earring hook, thread one group of discs. Finish this off with an extra felt disc and two beads before threading the second group and coming back round to the hook (Figures 87 and 88).

*Round disc necklace*

With little round discs of felt you can make endless variations of very beautiful necklaces. As it would take a very long time to cut out so many discs you can use small die-cuts or punches.

To do this, lay a piece of felt on a wooden board and bash out the discs with a punch and hammer. The red necklace in Figure 88 has discs of 1/4, 5/16, 3/8 and 1/2 in (6, 8, 10 and 12 mm). Thread a little bead between each disc. In the necklace shown, two discs of the same size are threaded together, so two discs of 1/4 in (6 mm), two of 5/16 in (8 mm), two of 3/8 in (10 mm), and two of 1/2 in (12 mm). After that the discs become smaller again. So for each colour group fourteen discs are used. Of course this can be varied. In the necklace in Figure 86 the colours are placed symmetrically; that is to say, the colour groups advancing from either side of the locket are always the same and only the very middle has a different colour.

*Earrings*

Follow the same principle to make matching earrings. In the earrings shown, all the colours used in the round disc necklace have been included in two groups, but you can of course make the earrings in one colour.

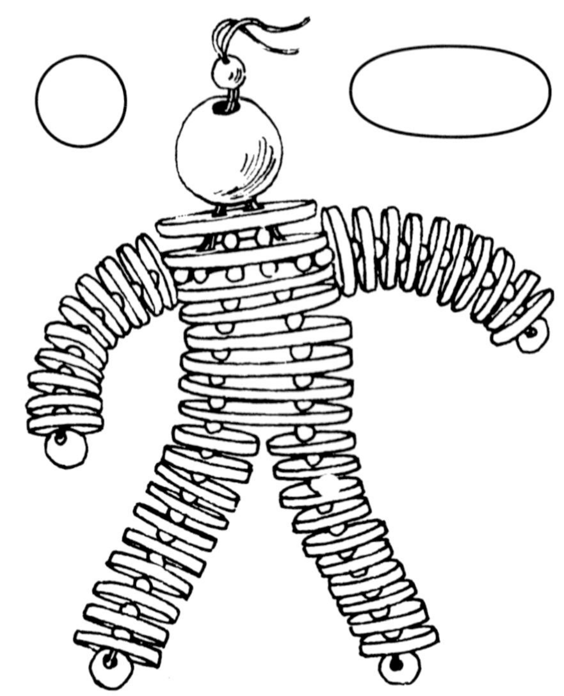

89 *Pattern for harlequin brooch*

## Harlequin brooch

*MATERIALS*

- Pieces of felt
- A large bead with a diameter of 5/8 in (15 mm)
- Three beads with a diameter of 3/16 in (5 mm)
- Two beads with a diameter of 1/4 in (7 mm)
- Small beads
- Thick coloured sewing thread
- Safety pin

*METHOD*

The harlequin in Figures 89 and 90 consists of round and oval discs of felt threaded together with a small bead between. The oval discs are about twice as wide as the round ones.

Choose the colour and cut out or punch out the round and oval discs.

The harlequin is made up of:

- 8 oval discs, 1 in (25 mm) wide for the body
- 10 round discs for each leg, 9/16 in (14 mm)
- 8 round discs for each arm, 1/2 in (12 mm)

Begin with the legs. Lay out the round discs in the desired order. Take a thread at least 12 in (30 cm) long and thread on a 1/4 in (7 mm) bead. The bead makes the foot. Bring the two ends of the thread together, and thread them through the eye of a needle. Now thread the first of the 9/16 in (14 mm) round discs on to the needle, followed by a bead, and then another round disc. Continue until you have threaded ten round discs and ten beads.

Put this first leg to one side with the needle still on it and repeat for the second leg.

Now take the first oval disc and bring the two threads of each leg through it, the threads from the left leg slightly to the left and the threads from the right leg slightly to the right of the centre of the disc. Then thread each pair of threads through a bead, and so on. When you come to the last oval but one, bring the threads more towards the middle of the oval, and even more so with the last oval (Figure 90).

Make the arms in the same way as the legs, but use the 3/16 in (5 mm) beads for the hands. The arms have two round discs then two beads in succession threaded upwards. Join the arms to the last but one oval of the body. Pass the thread through the middle of the last oval.

Now pass the threads of the arms and legs through the large bead (the head). Because the hole in this bead is quite big, fasten the threads on top of the head by threading on a smaller bead and then tying up all the loose ends.

The harlequin still needs his conical hat. Take a strip of felt 2 x 1 1/2 in (5 x 4 cm) and glue it on to the head. Trim it and sew it on at the back. The threads on which the whole harlequin has been strung can be left sticking out of the conical hat as a brush, but they will have to be secured with a few stitches.

Now sew the topmost discs of the arms to the back of the last oval. The arms will then hang well against the body.

Finally attach a safety pin to the conical hat and to the back of the oval discs to complete the brooch.

90 *Brooches from left: harlequin; gnome; butterfly; clown*

## *Clown brooch*

*MATERIALS*

- Pieces of felt
- White bead
- Red beads
- Safety pin
- Thin wire

*METHOD*

The head and arms of this clown are made with thin wire in the same way as the *Christmas gnome* on page 38 (Figure 40), but this time the frame is not brought down towards the lower body.

The pattern in Figure 91a–e consists of a jacket, a pair of trousers with feet and a cap. Cut out the jacket and make a cut in the back at the same time so that it can be laid around the upper body and sewn up. Cut out the trousers and sew the two parts together with blanket-stitch, sewing the feet between the two parts of the trouser legs at the same time. Sew the trousers on to the jacket and gather the waist in a bit. Glue the cap on to the head and embroider loops around the edge for decoration (Figure 90).

Finally fasten a safety pin vertically to the trousers.

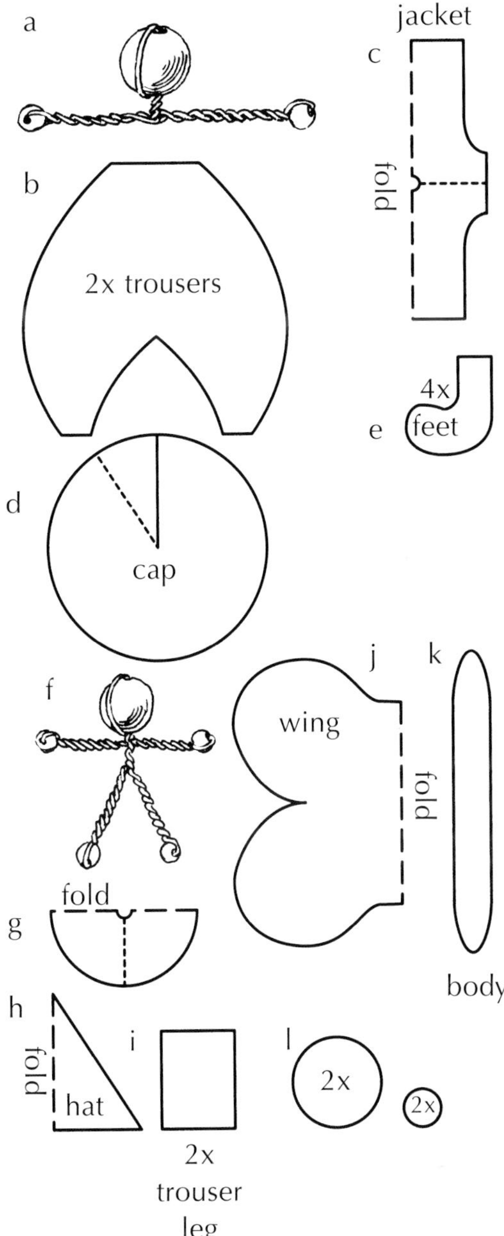


91 *Pattern for brooches*

## *Gnome brooch*

*MATERIALS*

- Pieces of felt
- Beads for the head, hands and feet
- Thin wire
- Safety pin

*METHOD*

This gnome is made in the same way as the *Christmas gnome* on page 38, but here the measurements are much smaller and the wire is not wrapped round with wool (Figures 90 and 91f–i).

Cut out the pattern pieces. Make the frame and sew the trousers around the legs. Cut the back open and make an opening for the neck. Wrap the smock around the arms and body and secure it.

Sew up the back seam of the conical hat and glue this on to the head.

Give the gnome a scarf out of a thin strip of yellow felt or woollen yarn. Finally sew a safety pin on to the back of the gnome.

## *Butterfly brooch*

*MATERIALS*

- Pieces of felt
- Safety pin

*METHOD*

See Figure 91j–l for the pattern for the butterfly. Cut out the wings and sew the round pieces of felt on to them. Finish off the edges with a decorative stitch, for instance blanket-stitch.

Take two pieces of felt for the body, sew these together and then on to the wings. Finally attach the safety pin to the underside of the butterfly (Figure 90).

# Gifts

## Doll in a matchbox

MATERIALS

- Pieces of felt
- Little wooden doll 1 1/4 in (3 cm) high
- Matchbox

METHOD

Cut out a piece of felt to fit exactly over the cover of the matchbox. Decorate the top part with embroidery or by sewing on a design such as a flower. Now glue the felt around the box cover.

Line the inside of the box with white felt.

Take a little wooden doll and dress the body with pink felt, gathering the piece of felt in at the top and bottom, so that it fits neatly around the neck.

Make the arms out of a piece of felt 1 1/2 x 1/2 in (4 x 1 cm). Fold the two ends and sew them together to make arms, sewing on tiny pieces of felt for the hands at the same time. Sew the middle of the strip on to the doll's back.

For the bonnet, take a piece of felt 1 x 5/8 in (2.5 x 1.5 cm), fold it in two, sew up the back and sew it on to the body.

Finally insert a small coloured piece of felt into the matchbox as a blanket.

92 *Doll in a matchbox*

93 *Gifts from left: bookmark; scissor case; comb case; purse*

## *Bookmark*

*MATERIALS*

- Pieces of felt

*METHOD*

A bookmark is very simple for children to make. Cut out a narrow strip of felt, for example 6 1/2 x 1 1/2 in (16 x 4 cm). Decorate it as you wish either by sewing on bits of felt or by embroidering it. You can finish off the sides with blanket-stitch (Figure 1 on page 8). You can also sew a thin piece of lining to the back to cover the stitches.

## *Comb case*

*MATERIALS*

- Pieces of felt

*METHOD*

Select a suitable comb and then cut out two pieces of felt to measure. Decorate one of the pieces, then sew the two pieces together with an ornamental stitch (Figure 1) leaving the top open.

## *Scissor case*

*MATERIALS*

- Pieces of felt
- Thin card

*METHOD*

Cut out the back of the case (Figure 94) twice, together with a piece of thin card 1/16 in (2 mm) smaller than the case.

Place the card between the two pieces of felt and sew these together with invisible stitches.

Now cut out the front and decorate it. Sew the back and front together and finish off the case by working a blanket-stitch around it (Figure 1).

## *Purse*

*MATERIALS*

- Pieces of felt
- Press studs or buttons

*METHOD*

The pattern for the purse in Figure 95 consists of a piece that forms the back and the flap, the front and a fastening for the flap. Cut out the back and embellish the front flap. Sew the inside of the flap and the front of the purse with blanket-stitch (Figure 1). Finally sew on one or two press studs.

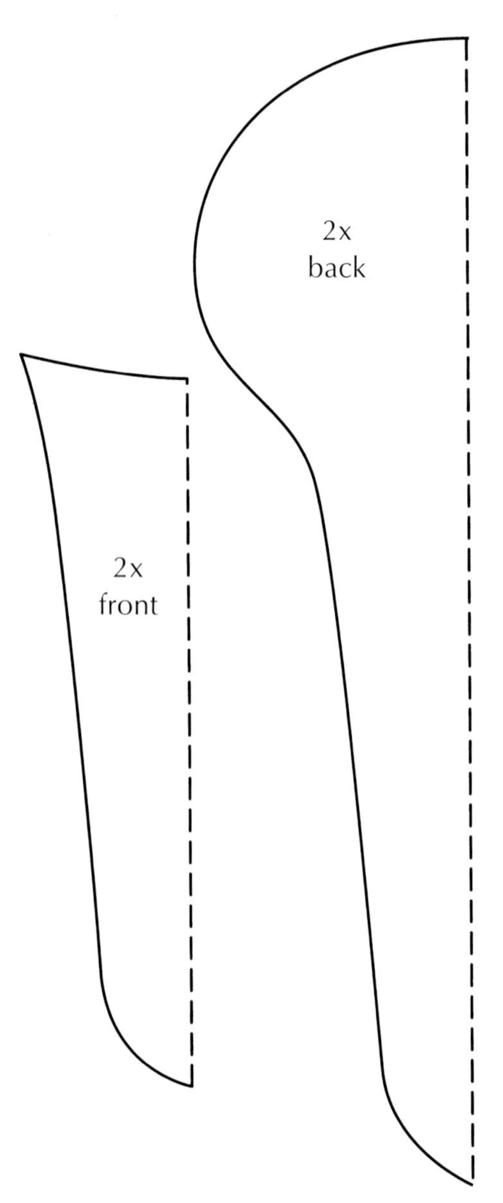


94 *Pattern for scissor case*

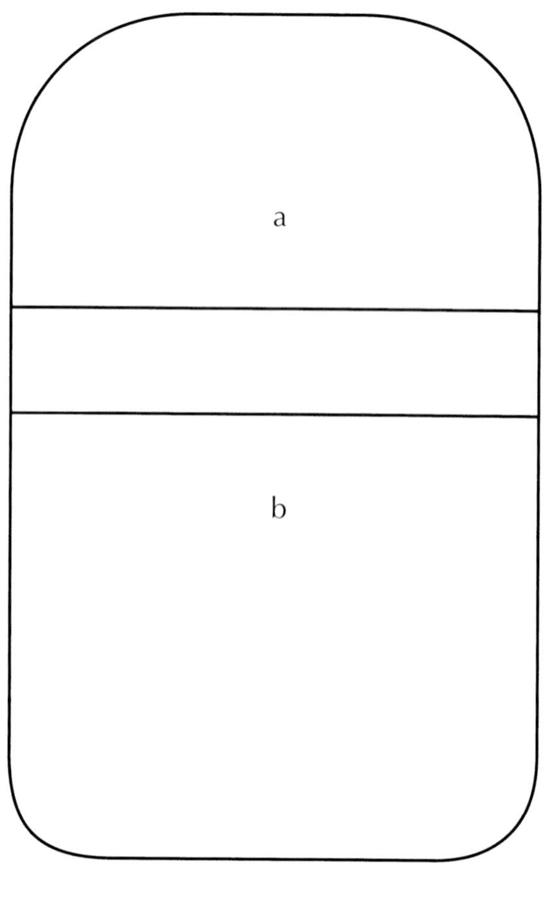


95 *Pattern for purse*

## *Decorating little boxes*

*MATERIALS*

- Pieces of felt
- Boxes

*METHOD*

You can buy wooden boxes of all sizes in craft shops. Choose one and glue some felt all over the outside of the bottom part of the box, leaving the top edge and the top parts of the sides clear so that the lid will fit. Experiment by trying on the lid to see exactly how much space needs to be left clear. Now cut out a piece of felt for the top and decorate it. You can embroider the felt or glue other bits of felt on to it, or you can do a combination of both.

The rose in Figure 96 consists of two discs cut in towards the middle in four places. Bring the points to the centre and secure them, thus making four petals. Finally sew the two discs with petals together and secure them to the piece of felt with a few stitches. Finally glue the felt on to the lid of the box and trim if necessary.

96 *Little decorated boxes*

97 *Egg-cosies*

## Egg-cosies

MATERIALS

- Pieces of felt
- Unspun wool
- Embroidery thread
- Beads

*Egg-cosy with flowers*

Figure 97 shows an egg-cosy with flowers. Cut the flowers out from a piece of felt and sew them on to the background. This egg-cosy can be made in many different ways, including working simply with embroidery thread on the felt.

*Patterned egg-cosy*

Cut out the pattern in Figure 100 and embellish one or both sides before sewing them together. You can do this by embroidering something on to them, or by sewing on small cut-out felt flowers.

*Hen egg-cosy*

Cut out the body from the pattern in Figure 98 twice, the wings twice, the beak twice and the comb once.

Sew the wings on to the body. Then sew the two halves of the hen's body together with buttonhole-stitch, sewing the comb between the two parts at the same time. Finish off the underside with buttonhole-stitch. Sew the two red beaks in position and fill the head with some wool.

Finally sew on two beads for the eyes.

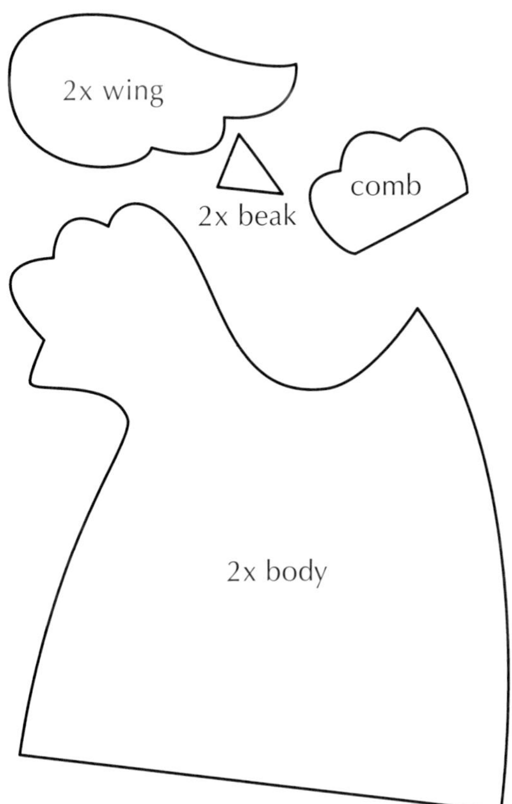


98 *Pattern for hen egg-cosy*

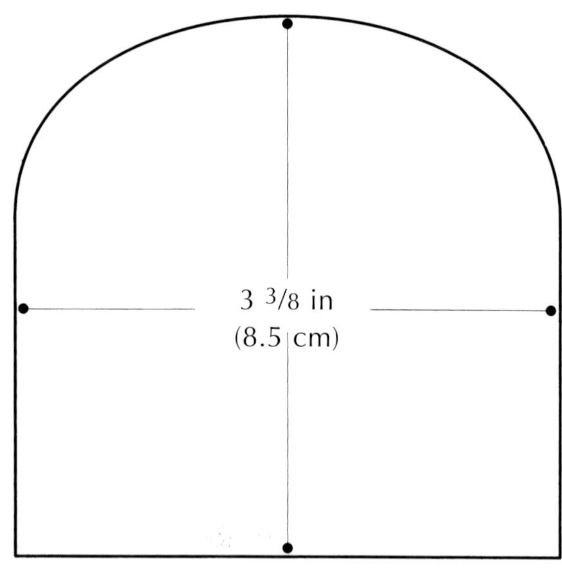


99 *Pattern for egg-cosy with flowers*

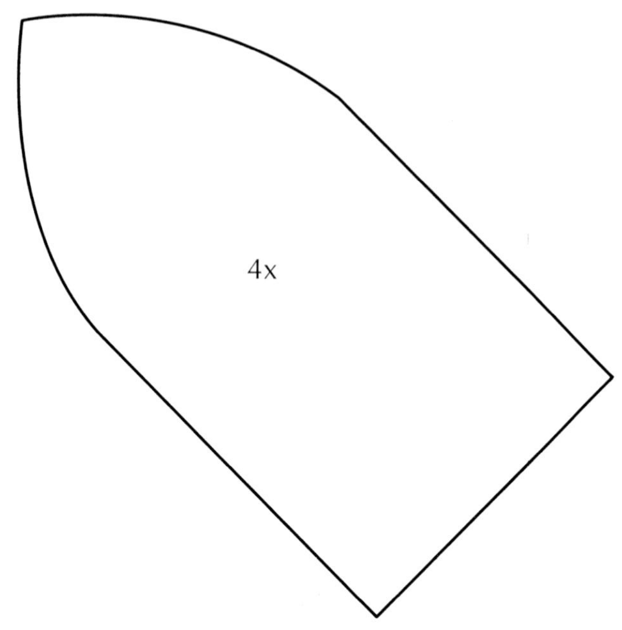


100 *Pattern for patterned egg-cosy*

# Materials

Some of the materials used in this book are easy to find, others may take some time to locate but should be available in good craft shops.

*Felt*

In the *Introduction* we declared our preference for pure woollen felt over acrylic or half-synthetic material. The latter can be very thin and the threads are too loosely woven, so while it is being sewn it can easily come apart. We would recommend Richard Wernekinck felt.

*Wooden dolls*

Unvarnished wooden dolls with cylindrical or tapered bodies are available in various sizes. There are also ready-made wooden dolls with moveable arms of wire and cord.

*Fabrics*

Cotton knit (white, pink and brown)
Cotton material
Teased, unspun wool, or carded fleece
Magic wool is dyed carded fleece. It should be fairly easy to find, but if not you can dye your own.

*Other items*

Pipe-cleaners
Unvarnished wooden beads are obtainable in several sizes and colours. Those used in this book have a diameter of 3/16, 1/4, 1/2, 5/8, 3/4, 1 1/4 in (5, 7, 12, 16, 20 and 32 mm).
Varnished wooden beads with a diameter of 1/8, 3/16, 1/4 in (4, 5 and 6 mm)
Necklace clasps
Earring hooks
Small bells
Wooden boxes
For thin card you can use thick cartridge paper.
Stiff card is 2 or 3-ply board (170–200 gsm).
Glue — a tube with a very thin nozzle is easiest to use.
A knitting Nancy

*Ironmongery*

Dies or punches 1/4, 5/16, 3/8, 1/2, 9/16 in (6, 8, 10, 12 and 14 mm)
Pinking shears
Iron rings with a diameter of about 3 1/2 in (9 cm)
Thin (copper) wire, thickness 1/32 in (0.8–1 mm)

Thomas and Petra Berger
ISBN 978–086315–721–9

Sybille Adolphi
ISBN 978–086315–718–9

Angelika Wolk-Gerche
ISBN 978–086315–678–6

Karin Neuschütz
ISBN 978–086315–719–6